Develop, Amplify & Direct Your Psychic Powers!

Any form of psychic development, even assisted by radionic or other psionic devices, is going to take some time. The methods in this book *shorten* the lag time between beginning psychic practice and achieving results. It bridges the gap between theory and practice which is all too prevalent in most books that purport to teach psychic development to their readers and it eliminates the nonsense which so often accrues to the study of these matters.

"A decade ago, I wrote a book on the electromagnetic spectrum and how energy is the key component to UFO events and psychic manifestations. Unfortunately, I expected my readers to have at least a high school level education in basic physics. An error that cost my publisher dearly. Now this upstart, Charles W. Cosimano, has written *Psychic Power*, and all I can do is grit my teeth and wish that I had written it. You don't even need a degree in advanced nuclear physics to understand it.

"This book tells you how to build simple devices that will enable you to utilize your psychic bio-energies. In another age, use of these forces was considered magic or witchcraft. Some people are still drawing circles on the floor and engaging in involved, exhausting rituals meant to accomplish the things that Mr. Cosimano achieves by just turning the knob on a little black box. He has managed to distill the wisdom of the ages in this book, and if you follow his instructions you might be able to change your whole life."

—John A. Keel
Director, Institute of Fortean Parapsychology

About the Author

CHARLES W. COSIMANO has been a teacher of psychic and magickal skills for more than ten years. He has an M. A. in History. More recently his interests have led him to become an active researcher and writer. He is a member of Phi Alpha Theta fraternity, and is the past chairman and current secretary of the Wheaton, Illinois, Study Center of the Theosophical Society in America, where he shares his home with two cats.

To Write to the Author

We cannot guarantee that every letter written to the author can be answered, but all will be forwarded. Both the author and the publisher appreciate hearing from readers, learning of your enjoyment and benefit from this book. Llewellyn also publishes a bi-monthly news magazine with news and reviews of practical esoteric studies and articles helpful to the student, and some readers' questions and comments to the author may be answered through this magazine's columns if permission to do is included in the original letter. The author sometimes participates in seminars and workshops, and dates and places are announced in *The Llewellyn New Times*. To write to the author, or to ask a question, write to:

Charles W. Cosimano
c/o THE LLEWELLYN NEW TIMES
P.O. Box 64383-097, St. Paul, MN 55164-0383, U.S.A.

Please enclose a self-addressed, stamped envelope for reply, or $1.00 to cover costs.

ABOUT LLEWELLYN'S NEW AGE PSI•TECH SERIES

Psychic Powers—we really understand very little about them. But, with an open mind, we have to admit the evidence that they do exist. We witness them in history, religion and myth, and we witness them all about us in both ordinary and extra-ordinary circumstances. We witness these amazing powers in psychic phenomena, radionics and psionics, in divination and dowsing, in healing and prophecy, and in miracles and mysteries of all kinds.

Over the whole history of humanity, these powers have been experienced and cultivated by shamans, magicians, witches and yogis, by holy (whole) men and women, and by people-in-need. Today, we also find them in the research laboratory and in the homes and offices of ordinary men and women seeking understanding of such phenomena and powers so that they can be directed and applied to self-improvement and attainment, *and for success.*

There are many *technologies* for developing and applying these little-known powers. But even when we lack under-standing of how something works, we can still find ways to apply it for our own benefit. Psychic Power lies dormant in everyone, and everyone—no matter who he or she is—can bring it out and use it. There are established technologies for psychic development and application, and there are simple "machines" (or interfaces) that can help develop and amplify your psychic powers.

In Llewellyn's Psi•Tech Series of books and tapes, we focus on these techniques and devices for tapping the many powers of the psyche, including those that join psyche and body, visible and invisible, life and Earth, humanity and cosmos. With this knowledge we seek better control over the per-sonal environment, adding a new and significant resource in dealing with the problems of everyday living—*and a means to understand and control the invisible factors that shape energies and events at community and planetary levels.*

Forthcoming from Charles Cosimano

Psionic Power

Llewellyn's New Age Psi•Tech Series

PSYCHIC POWER

Charles W. Cosimano

1989
Llewellyn Publications
St. Paul, Minnesota, 55164-0383, U.S.A.

International Standard Book Number: 0-87542-097-4
Library of Congress Catalog Number: 86-46304

(Originally published as Psionics 101)
First Edition, 1987
First Printing, 1987
Second Printing, 1987
Mass Market Edition, 1989

Cover Design: Brooke Luteyn
Illustrations: Nancy Benson
Cartoons: Jack Adair

Produced by Llewellyn Publications
Typography and Art property of Chester-Kent, Inc.

Published by
LLEWELLYN PUBLICATIONS
A Division of Chester-Kent, Inc.
P.O. Box 64383
St. Paul, MN 55164-0383, U.S.A.

Printed in the United States of America

Dedicated To:

Albert Abrams, who showed us where to begin
and to
Doc Smith for showing us where it can end.

Contents

INTRODUCTION

This book is about the ending of a monopoly. In spite of the millions of words that have been written on the subject of psychic powers and their development, relatively few people, even among those who have tried earnestly and with great perseverance, have succeeded in gaining any significant results. This book, if it is studied and applied, will change that. Why? Because everything in this book is true. Every device I am going to teach you works. They have worked for me and they have worked for others. They will, if you are willing to give them the time and patience, work for you.

So let me begin with what I am *not* going to do. I am not going to waste my time with legends and fairy tales. I do not believe them and I will not insult your intelligence by expecting you to. Everything I will teach you in this book can be verified by experiment on your part. You are going to become powerful in the truest sense of the word. There are going to be times when you will be so powerful and things will work so well that you will wonder if you have somehow stepped into a comic book.

The very first thing you must get into your mind is this:

Psychic power lies dormant in everyone, and everyone, no matter who he is, can bring it out and use it.

1

There is nothing miraculous about this power. There is nothing even supernatural about it. It simply exists and could be used by everyone in the world if only they would be willing to take the time and trouble to learn how to use it and then sit back and wait for it to work.

There are machines in use now that can develop and amplify your psychic powers.

In this book you will learn about the famous Radionic Boxes which are right now in common use in Great Britain and which have powers so awesome, yet so simple that the medical profession in this country refuses to believe that it can work, in spite of the overwhelming evidence that it does. You will learn how to make and use these boxes, not only for healing, but for all psychic works. You will learn how to use these wonderful machines to send messages even around the world!

I will teach you the proper way to meditate to bring health and friendship and riches into your life!

No funny words or smelly incense required. I will teach you an amazingly simple and effective way to meditate which has worked so marvelously well for others and will work for you—*without fail*!

You will learn of the magnificent relationship which exists between everything in the universe and how to use this relationship!

Did you know that the Sun and the stars are all part of the same, one, thing? Did you know that everything which exists in the entire universe is related to everything else? In this book you will learn of the secret of that relationship and how, by its very nature, it will work for you.

You will learn how to uncover the secret thoughts of others and how to control those thoughts!

The mind of every man and woman is but an open book to anyone who is willing to learn a few simple techniques. You will never be fooled or deceived again if you follow the instructions in this book.

You will learn the great mystery which underlies all success in the psychic realm!

There is a key, a hidden key, kept secret for thousands of years which, if properly used and understood, will virtually insure the success of any endeavor. This key is desire, and I will teach you how to channel desire into the proper directions for maximum well-being and power.

You will learn of the true existence of unseen friends and how they can help you!

This is *not* the stuff of fairy stories. Those who inhabit the invisible worlds are not the evil bugaboos and monsters that many would have you believe. They are true friends and benefactors. I will teach you why you should contact them and the way to do it without fear.

You will learn how to manipulate the psychic energies of the universe to insure your health and well-being!

As a part of the universe, you are entitled to perfect health, and while everyone has certain physical defects, I will teach you to be as healthy as possible and how to give the blessings of good health to your friends.

I will give you the design for a miraculous helmet which will amplify your thoughts!

This is not something out of a science-fiction story. The Psionic Amplifier Helmet is easy to build and I will tell you how to do it.

You will discover the power of total psychic bombardment!

I will teach you how to so command the forces of the universe that you will become a psychic Power Master, able to impose your will upon your environment, rather than be a mere pawn in the games of others.

Anyone, and I mean that quite literally, from the smallest child to the oldest adult, can use this power. It is a terrible thing to say, but this power is so easy to use that we must conclude that those who fail to use it do so either because of ignorance of the power and its uses, or because of fear. Ignorance can be excused, for not everyone has the opportunity to learn, or the material is presented in such a fashion as to make learning impossible. There is, however, no excuse for fear.

There are those, unpleasant as this is to say, who stand to profit by keeping humanity in fear of the psychic realms. Some do so from religious motives. They would like you to think that all psychic power comes from a cartoon creature called the Devil. I will confess to having little use for that argument, and firmly hold the opinion that anyone who is foolish enough to believe it is a good customer for the used bridge salesman. Then there are those who feel more directly threatened, and in some cases rightly so. The liar has much to fear from the one who can detect the lie.

Finally, there are those who must have the universe and all it contains fit their neat theories. Their minds are like steel traps, and once they close upon a matter they never open again. These would call psychic power a fraud because it does not fit the equations. Ignore that argument. In the early years of the nineteenth century, when railroads were first proposed, a London magazine ridiculed the idea of men travelling at forty miles per hour and claimed that the idea was as preposterous as putting a man on top of a rocket and shooting him at the moon.

For those of you, who for one reason or another, have some doubts in this matter, do not feel that I am ignoring your worries. I had them myself once.

I was raised by staunch materialists who refused to believe in anything which could not be perceived by the usual five senses. I, quite naturally given the circumstances, assumed that this was the case and at that time I was supported in that view by my teachers and society at large. Then the occult revolution began and I found myself caught up in it, not so much out of belief but simply because I discovered that girls were interested in it and some knowledge of the psychic realm was sure to impress them. Well, it did just that. It also began to impress me. Strange as it may seem, I found myself believing my own propaganda and began to experiment in earnest.

This is not to say that I had not had psychic experiences before. When I was twelve, I was given a battery-operated lie detector for a Christmas present. It did not take long for me to discover that I could, merely by willing it, make the needle of the machine move as I directed it. By accident I had learned of what is now called biofeedback, but in those days nobody had heard of the word. But something else began to happen. I discovered that while playing with the machine I began to have what I later learned were pre-cognitive experiences. I could, in some instances, know what questions were to be asked on tests at school.

From doing funny things with the little lie detector, I went on to experimenting with telepathy. That was not, I will admit, entirely successful and thus I was not entirely impressed. But I pressed on, now motivated by some curiosity, in an almost total vacuum of knowledge on the subject of the psychic. For example, in spite of my biofeedback experiments, I had no knowledge of the role of relaxation in psychic work, and meditation was virtually unheard of. But I persevered, sometimes succeeding, more often failing, and making some spectacular blunders along the way.

I was given a Ouija Board for a present, but never considered it anything more than a toy, in spite of the fact that it told me many useful things. It was not until I began to experiment with the pendulum that I began to take the subject of the psychic seriously, and not just as a rather silly set of parlor games.

I even acquired a small book in which the radionic devices which will be such an important part of this book were described in enough detail that it would have been a simple matter for me to make one. Yet I found the idea so unbelievable that I put the book aside for many years. I regret that decision now, because if I had taken the material more seriously I would have saved myself literally years of effort.

What I am trying to make you understand with this little confession is this. You may have tried any number of systems for developing psychic abilities and failed at all of them, or if lucky, may have had some little success but nothing so magnificent that you are about to put the Gifted Reader sign outside your door. You keep reading of Mr. X. and how he meditated his way to a million dollars in a week, but you are still trying to get the rent paid on time. After enough failures, you are probably ready to believe that this "psychic stuff" is all bunk.

In short, you may have tried everything and found that your life is still a mess. Well, my friend, take heart. If you follow my instructions, your life may still be a mess, but it will be a manageable mess, and as you continue to follow my instructions you will find that more and more of the time you will be gaining the upper hand over your environment. And that, my friend, is what the purpose of developing this power is. You are gaining the means to influence your environment.

Do not be deterred by the concept of power. There was a time, not so long ago, when power was looked down upon. Thankfully, that time is fading into a soon-to-be-forgotten past, but the mentality which created it still lingers, and it lingers because of a basic misunderstanding of what power is. Power is, very simply, the means to accomplish an end—any end. The only difference is the type of power employed and the type of person employing it. Economic power is one form, and those who possess it use it to achieve social and political ends. Electrical power is different in that it is natural rather than social in origin, but it is power, nonetheless, and is used to accomplish mechanical ends. Both are used by individuals to cause certain results from their use. Psychic power is not a bit different in that regard. It can be used to get results, and in this book it is results that we are interested in. What separates psychic power from other forms is that its existence is not yet universally recognized, and unlike other forms, is not subject to any control outside of the individual using it. There is no legislature in the world that can control the use of psychic abilities. No company can claim a monopoly. The psychic abilities of an individual rest sovereign in that individual and there is no power outside of that person which can prevent him from using them.

So much for the introductory comments. Start reading and get to work. By the time you have finished everything in this book you should be well on your way to becoming a psychic power-master, able to bend the world, or at least parts of it, to your will.

1

Psychic Energy

What is this energy we will be using? It is an energy that exists in unlimited supply. It is an energy that can be manipulated to cause results and thus becomes power. You must understand that there is nothing new about the energy itself. Like all other manifestations of energy in the physical world, this energy has been around since the dawn of creation. In fact, it is not stretching the point to claim that it was the force of creation itself, for if anything in this universe can be defined as the stuff of which Gods are made, this energy most certainly is.

It has definite properties, just as heat, light and other energies have that we normally deal with every day.

1) It exists in and through *all* things. There is not a single living or non-living object in the entire physical universe which is not totally permeated by this energy, be it the most inert clump of stone to the brightest star; everything contains this energy.

2) It can be made, or at least observed to, travel with all other forms of energy, particularly light and electromagnetic transmissions.

3) It can be polarized and will behave much the same as light does, including passing through lenses and being reflected by mirrors.

4) It has been observed to emanate from the entire human body, but most particularly from the fingertips and eyes. Other important emissions points are the palms of the hands, the center of the forehead and the top of the head. It has also been claimed that the soles of the feet are strong emitters of this energy, but I have some personal doubts as to that.

5) Because of its peculiar relation to electro-magnetic energy, it can be carried on any conductor of that energy, such as ordinary wire.*

As bizarre as this may seem, it was proven by an experiment which you may easily duplicate. In the patent application for his radionic device to detect minerals, T. Galen Hieronymus described a novel method for feeding plants. He took two groups of seeds and planted them in separate boxes in a darkened basement. One box was the control and was not treated in any way other than to plant them. (While the patent does not state the fact, we may assume the plants were watered.) The other plants were treated in the same way, with the exception that onto the plants, wires were attached and led out to the outside of the building where they were in turn connected to metal plates which were exposed to light. The result? The plants that were wired to the outside grew to be quite strong and healthy, while the control group was, as you

---

* Sheila Ostrander and Lynn Schroeder, *Handbook of Psychic Discoveries* (New York, New York: Berkely Publishing Corp., 1974), p. 169.

would expect, not strong and anything but healthy.*

6) Because this energy is present in all matter, it can be stored in all matter. It can be concentrated in objects and then released at will. The small devices made by the Czech engineer Robert Pavlita are proof of this property. One of his devices will attract objects under water, whether they are magnetic or not. Another can even be used to run a small motor.

7) The mind of an individual can be trained to operate this energy. Remember, just as this energy is not new, neither is its use. It goes back to the first intelligent humans to walk on this planet. Legend and popular fiction would have us believe that Atlantis was destroyed because of the misuse of this energy, but Atlantis may only be legend. We do know that primitives in isolated parts of the world still use this energy on a regular basis. Of course, much of the stories are just that, stories, made up for the joy of fooling the crazy anthropologists and giving creative answers to their questions. But even taking that into account, we are left at a loss to explain the phenomena which occur, unless, of course, we are willing to accept the fact of psychic energy. But it is in the relationship that exists between the psychic energy and the physical world that we have our greatest interest, as far as this book is concerned.

We can use the human body as an example of this relationship. The true physical nature of the human body is known to everyone, right down to the fact that even the atoms that make it are well defined. What is

---

* Edward W. Russell, *Report on Radionics* (Suffolk, U.K.: Neville Spearman, 1979), p. 99.

less known, and quite hard to accept at first, is the fact that the whole body, right down to its subatomic particles, is put together something like a skyscraper. Now, for those of you who may not know, a skyscraper is a building constructed somewhat different from the traditional way of putting up strong walls and then working from that. It is a framework of girders, and the building is quite literally hung on the framework. The human body, in fact all matter, has a framework as well. In the human this is called the etheric body, and it is made up of the same stuff which constitutes psychic energy.

Yes, strange as this may seem, this energy of which we have been speaking and which has caused so much discussion and difficulty is the very building material of the physical world. And this is the reason for the statement that it is included in all matter, for if it is the stuff that forms the material world, how can anything in the material universe exist separate from it?

The body is first formed of etheric matter before it takes on the physical form. How can we assert this? We have the unpleasant evidence of the phantom pain.

If something drastic happens to the body of a person, such as the loss of a limb in an accident, the etheric limb is still present. The individual will feel intense pain in the place where the missing limb would be, but there is no limb there and there are no nerves to carry the pain. But let a person be born with a part missing, and the pain never occurs. Why? The etheric body never formed that part and thus does not respond to its lack. But the presence of the phantom pain yields more information about the relationship between the etheric and the physical bodies than this. Remember, there are no nerve endings in an amputated limb. They are gone. You cannot cut a finger that is not there! Yet pain is felt, and felt strongly. How is this to be? There is a functional relationship between the etheric body and the human nervous system which enables the pain to be felt by the brain. The energy travels with electromagnetic energy, so it is able to carry the same information as the physical energy. The etheric nerves feel the pain, even if the physical nerves are not present, and act for all practical purposes as physical nerves to carry the information to the brain that something is very wrong.*

It is this capacity to carry information which is of primary importance to us in our work in this book. And now I have to ask you to take a bit of a leap with me. We will operate under the assumption that there is an all-pervasiveness to this energy, and thus the etheric body of one individual is functionally connected to the etheric body of every other individual by this same psychic energy, and this connection is the means by which psychic power operates.

Once energy is placed into the etheric body, it can be transmitted to any other etheric body and thence to the nervous system of any given individual. It will operate in this way the same as the etheric body does when transmitting a phantom pain. It is, by this means, not only possible to send specific thought

---

* Phil Allen, Alastair Bearne and Roger Smith, *Energy, Matter and Form* (Boulder Creek, Calif.: University of the Trees Press, 1979), pp. 13-14.

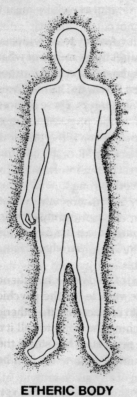

**ETHERIC BODY
PRODUCED BY
BIRTH DEFECT**

ETHERIC BODY

messages to other people, but also to send feelings and even physical responses. Remember, when you transmit any psychic message, you will be transmitting to the physical nervous system as well, by means of the etheric connection.

Not only can you transmit directly to individuals, but you can also transmit indirectly by means of what are normally considered inanimate objects. For proof of this, we must return to Robert Pavlita and his machines which he calls Psychotronic Generators. These devices come in various shapes and sizes for various functions and they all have one thing in common. Pavlita is able to concentrate energy into them by thought, and the generators release the energy. He has thus far kept the secret of how he is able to do this from all but his daughter,* but the demonstrations of his devices have convinced most that they are genuine, if a bit mysterious. Later I will tell you how to make a similar device for yourself that will work. But what happens when Pavlita charges one of his generators?

When Pavlita charges one of his devices, his etheric body, which is acting as the vehicle for the psychic energy being used, comes into contact with the etheric structure (it would be stretching the point to call it a body) of the generator. The generator thus stores the energy being placed there until it is time for it to be released.

There is one final property of this energy that you must remember. Energy cannot die. It can be used up or transformed into other energy, but it is always there in one form or another. It never ceases to exist.

---

*Ostrander and Schroeder, 217-218.

Now, as your body is made up originally of energy, is it such a large jump to consider the fact that your thoughts also have their origin in energy? And if your thoughts originate in your mind, must that not too exist originally as energy? So, we are forced to come to a logical conclusion that if energy is eternal and your mind is energy, then your mind must in some way be eternal. And if your mind is eternal, so must the mind, the thoughts and the knowledge of everyone *else* be eternal. All death is the ceasing of the functioning of the physical body, something like the car breaking down forcing the driver to walk. Just because the car no longer works does not mean the driver has stopped working.

Of course, it may be that with the passage of long periods of time certain transformations of the energy body might take place; for energy *can* be transformed, but we are not concerned with that. What we *are* concerned with is the fact that the energy bodies of those who have lost their physical vehicles still exist and function, which means that the minds of those individuals also continue to function.

Now the conclusion from this must be obvious. If the etheric body of an individual can be used to impart information to rock and metal, then it should also be able to contact the dead. And indeed it can. Thomas Edison had as one of his pet but uncompleted projects a machine to speak with the dead, a psychic telephone, so to say. The idea still holds fascination for many, and such a device is possible. In fact, I will show you how to make one and I guarantee it to be unlike anything ever to pop up in a dimly lit seance room.

So now you know what type of energy you will

be working with. Keep the properties and functions of it in mind as you work. As you progress with the development both of your powers and the machines I will teach you about, remember that everything in this book is based on the nature of this energy, but also remember that the last word on it is yet to be written. In many ways we are in much the same position as the early experimenters in electricity were during the 1700's. We know that there is something called psychic energy. We have tons of evidence as to its effects and use. We have finally managed to deduce some of its properties. But, due to the primitive nature of both our knowledge and our technology, we are just beginning to find practical uses for it. After all, Benjamin Franklin must have known that the power of lightning could be used to light homes and power machinery. But he was forced to be content to stop it from burning down houses, no small feat in a day when the local clergy were convinced that lightning was a sign of divine wrath, and thus were certain that the lightning rod was blasphemous in the extreme. In fact, it is a good rule to follow to remember that if anything comes along which will improve life, some church will oppose it.

Thus if the things I will teach you to do in this book seem odd, or the machines primitive, remember that we are standing on one shore, trying vainly to see the opposite one and hoping that someday someone will build the boat that can get us there.

But we don't build a boat without first learning what will float, so go on to the next chapter and get started. There is much to be done.

2

Power Meditation

Now that I have explained to you something about the energies we will be using, it is time to get to work and learn how to use them. We will begin by studying the time-honored practice of meditation. Now, I can already hear you groaning "Not that old nonsense again! Why can't I just make my machines and get on with the fun stuff?" Well, my friend, you are certainly free to skip over to the chapter on building your devices, but I would advise you to read this one first and try some of the exercises herein. You will find, as I have found and many others have as well, that the successful use of psychic power, even mechanically assisted power, comes from first having a clear mind which is able to concentrate on the use of the machines. Also, there are many things for which a machine is not even required; simply using meditative techniques can bring about the desired results.

When I say meditation, I do not mean twisting yourself into some ridiculous posture that intelligent beings were never made to be in, nor do I mean indulging in such foolishness as living in a cave and eating nothing but brown rice. To be frank, I have little patience with those who do advocate such things.

What I do mean is that my meditation has the ability to calm the body and the mind, to concentrate on a given subject and to see certain things in your mind's eye. It is not necessary to practice these things every day, but some sort of regular schedule is advisable, and you should do your best to follow it.

You should begin by considering your own body, particularly your breathing. This is not difficult, merely find yourself a comfortable chair in which you can sit without falling asleep. You should also try to find a place where you cannot be disturbed, not because disturbances are particularly dangerous, but because you may find yourself enjoying the relaxed state so much that to be brought suddenly out of it by an offending family member may cause you to lose your temper.

Once you have found your spot, sit quietly for about ten minutes at a time. That is how you start; just by sitting quietly, doing nothing, and while sitting try to notice how your body reacts. Notice that twitch in your right leg. You cannot help but be aware of an itch in your scalp, so do not hesitate to scratch it. Feel your lungs filling with air, rising and falling, pushing out your rib cage and letting it fall back in.

As you sit, you will notice all these things. Your body has certain places that are naturally tense. You will hear things you would normally ignore. That is really not so strange. We have all had the experience of trying to go to sleep only to be constantly reminded of some slight creak in the house which during the activity of our waking hours we would not even notice because our minds were too busy to notice them.

Pay very close attention to all these things and you will discover something interesting. The more you listen to your own body, the less you are bothered by the thoughts of the day. This is because your conscious mind can only handle one piece of data at a time. If you are studying intently, you will not pay attention to the smell of smoke until the fireman breaks down the door. The more you practice, the more effective your mind becomes at blocking out unwelcome stimuli.

Do this for a week or two. After that, you should proceed to calm your mind still further, and to do this you will use what is called a mantra. Don't panic! A mantra is just a set of sounds which you think in order to keep out other thoughts.

Sit comfortably. Try to breathe regularly, in a set rhythm, but do not become overly concerned about that. Your body has its own rate of breathing and if you try too hard to upset that rate, your body will get upset at you. I remember when I thought it was necessary to breathe in a certain way in order to attain a fully relaxed state. The results were exactly the opposite. My heart began to pound and I had to abandon the exercise for fear that I was on my way to a coronary. Just breathe naturally, not forcing yourself into any set pattern. Your body knows what it is doing, so trust it.

Notice each time you breathe how you inhale and exhale. If you are *not* doing that, start quickly or you will be dead and will have no further need of this book. Now, pick a couple of sounds. The Indians, or at least some of them, use the sounds *so* and *hum*. These are an approximation of the noise the breath makes as it enters and leaves the body. They also have the advantage of being easy to remember. It works like this. As you inhale, think the sound *So*. As you exhale, think the sound *Hum*. Just do this while you sit, and you will notice that by doing this you block out wandering thoughts which can disturb you, and, if they are about something unpleasant like bills, make you too upset to continue.

Practice this for about a month. You should, by the end of that time, discover a few definite changes in yourself. First, you should be able to think more clearly. Second, you should be more relaxed in your everyday life. This is not to say that you will not have any upsets; far from it, but you should be able to handle most of them better than you do now. Finally, you will be able to blot from your mind any unnecessary worries that might creep in. Worry, incidentally, is one thing which is not only unnecessary, but also dangerous. In the Bible, Jesus said that no man ever added a day to his life by worrying about it and he was right. The less you worry, the better off you will be.

But the principal reason I am taking the time to teach you this technique is not to improve your mental health. That is a side benefit (no extra charge). Meditation has the added advantage of putting your mind into condition to be able to manipulate psychic energy.

Why should this be? Understand that your mind is constantly putting out this energy. Every second, some part of your consciousness is transmitting into the etheric body and thence to the psychic world. Most of these transmissions come to nothing because there is not enough energy behind them to hold them together. The thought message goes out and immediately dissipates into the ether. It is like a clump of earth. When the clump is moist, it has a cohesion which will hold it together in a breeze. But let it dry, and the wind pushes at it, pulling away small parts until there is nothing left but the dust floating in the air, capable of getting the laundry dirty, but little else. So it is with the energy of our thoughts. It is only by being able to concentrate this energy that we are able to make it do any work. To use another analogy, there may be more kinetic energy in a good rainstorm than in a slow-moving stream, but the stream can be made to run a turbine while the falling rain, in individual drops, does nothing but nourish the shrubbery.

With that in mind we will now learn how to make thought-forms and to concentrate our psychic energy. This is going to take some time and practice, so I advise you to be patient. In the realm of the psychic there are no more free lunches than anywhere else.

In order to concentrate, you must first have something to concentrate on, and by that I mean a concrete, physical object rather than some abstract idea. Take a pencil, for example, and study it. Try to notice as many different things about it as you can. What is it for? What is it made of? What other things can it be used for besides its intended purpose? All the things which make it a pencil rather than a cabbage should be considered. Now sit back in your chair and relax. Begin your mantra like you always do, repeating *so* and then *hum*, breathing in and then out, completely naturally, until you feel that you have somehow managed to cut yourself off from the rest of the world.

Continue in this state and close your eyes. Now comes the hard part. Try to see the pencil in your mind's eye and hold it there as long as you can. You should find the experience to be a little disappointing at first because the pencil will refuse to stay put. Remember to try to really *see* the pencil, not merely recite the word "pencil." The image will flit in and out, with different parts appearing and disappearing. You will see the lead and then the eraser. You may see nothing but the name of the company printed on its side, only to have the image leave completely and be replaced by the smiling face of your first girl friend. This is all perfectly natural and is an excellent indication of the way the mind works. It also explains why it is so difficult to create a working thought-form. Now you know why all those writers and teachers who simply tell their pupils to visualize something are all wet. If it is this difficult to hold the simple image of a pencil in a prepared mind, how much more trouble would a completely untrained person have holding the image of a person or complicated object? Now you understand why most of those books sold on this subject failed in their purpose. They made demands which were impossible for an untrained person to fulfill, and also neglected the preliminary training.

Continue to work on the pencil, and above all else do not be discouraged by failure. It took me some years to master the technique, but I was less than committed. I wish I could tell you just exactly how long it will take to get this down to the point where you can do it at will; unfortunately everyone is different. The best advice I can give is to keep at it.

After you feel that you are able to hold the image of the pencil in your mind for, let us say, five minutes, you may proceed to other things. Take a coin and do the same thing with it as you did with the pencil. You will find that once the ability comes, it grows ever easier with practice, and it will take you far less time to hold a complete image of the coin than it did for the pencil.

Once you have sufficiently mastered this practice to your own satisfaction, you will be ready to create your first thought-form. What is a thought-form? A thought-form is a hard clump of psychic material, as strange as that idea may seem, and in the pre-physical world in which it functions it will be as solid as a rock, but a rock which will be constantly radiating energy, and it will do so until the energy which is fed into it as its creation is exhausted.

Sit comfortably. You must now prepare yourself to work with the stuff of the psychic world, and that means following certain forms, just as working in the physical needs some preparation. Begin to meditate. Use the mantra to clear your mind of the troubles of the day. There must be no outside interference with this, so get anything that will cause you to lose your concentration out of your head. Do *not* consciously will such unwelcome thoughts to leave; that will only impress them further. It is much better to simply ignore them and think your mantra.

Continue with your mantra, feeling your body detach itself from its surroundings. You should have your eyes closed. If they are open, you may actually notice a change in your perspective of the room you

**THE ETHERIC MATTER COALESCES
INTO A THOUGHTFORM**

are in. Continue in this state as long as you wish.

Now you must begin to visualize. In your mind, see a beam of light coming into your body from the ceiling. Concentrate this light in your body, feeling yourself being filled with the light as if you were a bottle being filled with water. Hold that light in. It may help to say to yourself something like "I fill myself with the energy of the universe."

Now see this energy forming a ball in front of you. Keep packing the light into the ball so that it becomes more and more solidified. Make a wish, any wish, and put it into the ball. Then release it like a cannon shot into the void.

Now for a word of caution. You will probably get exactly what you ask for, even if you do not know why you are asking for it. Therefore, it is of absolute importance that you *never*, under *any* circumstances, create a thought-form when you are feeling depressed. All this will do is to make matters worse. That is why worry is such a bad habit, because worry is a form of concentration, and thus the things you worry about are made more likely to happen.

But do not dwell on such unpleasantness. You have made your first thought-form, and if you have done it correctly, should notice some tangible results. Let us now consider how you may use this new-found ability for your benefit.

One of the most important things you have learned with this practice is not merely the creation of lumps of psychic matter. You have also learned a technique which can be used to program your own etheric body to make it attract to you those things you desire. If, even after all this, you still have doubts about the existence of your etheric body, here is a simple experiment that you can do to prove to yourself that it does, in fact, exist. All that you have to do is to take your right hand and move it very slowly about an inch over the back of your left hand. Did you notice a slight feeling as if there were an air current in between your two hands? That feeling was your etheric body.

Now go over to a plant, any plant will do. Hold your hand out over the leaf nearest you, but do not touch it. Now, slowly move your hand across the leaf. The leaf will move, following your hand. That was your etheric body again, this time moving against the plant. But you are going to do more than that. You are going to learn how to control your own etheric body so that it can effectively extend itself to touch other people at a distance.

As you sit in your chair, begin to meditate as you always do. When you feel yourself relaxed, close your eyes and try to see yourself. Sometimes it helps to sit before a mirror when you begin until you get the visualized image down. Remember, visualization takes time to learn, and you may find that you have more difficulty with this than you did with your previous exercises. Do not let yourself become discouraged because it *will* come if you keep at it. It is something like learning to drive. At first, everything is an effort, but with practice, it comes as naturally as walking.

When you are able to see yourself in your mind and hold the image, you will be ready for the next step. To this point, you have only been visualizing your physical body. Now you will add the etheric body to the image. You do this by seeing yourself surrounded by a glowing light. It does not have to be too strong a glow at first. You can, if you wish, build that up later. While you do this, think to yourself these words, "I am seeing my body. This image is my body, my physical body and my psychic body. I see the energy field around my body."

Continue this until you can, at will, sit and visualize the energy field of your own body. When you are able to do this, you will be ready for the next step.

Sit and visualize your body with the energy field of your etheric body shining around it, making your body look like a human-shaped neon light. See the light coming down from the ceiling, bathing your etheric body, making it glow even brighter. Know that the glow of the etheric body is the radiating energy of that body, and everything that this energy touches must be affected by it in some way. You are, for all practical purposes, setting up a magnetic field around your body which will attract to you that which you desire.

You can use this power of attraction to bring you companionship and romance.

Everyone fears loneliness. Even the hermit in his mountain retreat secretly wishes to return to society and have people around him. This is inherent in the nature of the human species. Man is a gregarious animal. Like the wolf, he runs best in a pack, and while he can function alone, does not wish to. But the way our society is put together, the isolated individual has become the rule rather than the exception. Even when we are in a group, we feel basically alone, totally isolated from our fellows. And when the desire for a mate is combined with that essential aloneness we feel doubly distressed. You, however, now have the basic tools with which you can bring companionship into your life.

Begin by programming your etheric body to bring you a partner. You sit and meditate like always. Visualize first your body and then add your etheric body. Bring in light, causing your etheric body to glow as brightly as you are able. Watch the energy streaming down. As you see it pouring into you, feel yourself radiating energy back. Repeat this to yourself: "I am the source of love and attraction. My etheric body is now tuned as a magnet which must attract love to me. Everyone who comes within range of my etheric body will be attracted to me. I am a source of power, and no one can resist me."

Your etheric body is now charged like a battery, and like a battery is ready to put out energy when you release it. To release it you simply use your imagination.

Prepare your etheric body. While meditating, imagine yourself moving through a group of people, preferably those whom you wish to attract. As you move by them responding to you with interest, not even knowing why they are interested.

This exercise will serve a double purpose. You have now programmed your etheric body to work on the etheric bodies of other people. You are also training your own mind to put that body to work when you are in the presence of others. Eventually it will become almost a reflex response inside your mind, and the response will work unconsciously as well as consciously. Your energy field will begin to function in the desired manner automatically to bring to you the companionship of those you desire.

You may also use a thought-form to bring about the same results. In this case, it is best to have a particular subject in mind, though it is not necessary. Assume you have a given individual you would like to meet, but the opportunity never seems to arise. Go back a couple of pages to the description of how to create a working thought-form. Follow the instructions, but this time give the ball of energy a name, such as Egbert or whatever. As you visualize this ball hanging in the air in front of you, tell it what you wish it to do, as clearly and as concisely as possible. Never create a thought-form to do more than one thing. They are not very smart, and you will only confuse it. After you have created your ball, named it and given it its instructions, send it on its way. It should hit your subject immediately and begin to work.

When you use the thought-form, it is good to remember that it can run out of power before the work is completed. Therefore, you may have to send more than one after a few days, and you should not be hesitant about doing this. A little reinforcement never hurts.

Once you have mastered these methods, you may go on to other things. As I have told you, the energy we work with is transmitted best by two parts of the body, the eyes and the hands. You must now learn how to control the flow of this power through these parts so that it can be directed at will. The method involved is quite easy, though it may take a little time to do it right, so do not be discouraged if your initial experiments bring little or no results. In time they *will* work.

As you meditate, see your etheric body. Now try to see those parts of the body where the energy radiates the strongest. You will notice that one hand tends to put out more than the other, and one eye likewise is more conducive to radiating energy. You are going to have to balance this if you wish to be truly effective, so begin to draw energy into your body. Feel the energy flow into your body and try to direct it so that the flow from the eyes and hands is even. You do this by seeing the energy as light and visualizing an even stream of power proceeding out from each location. Repeat this exercise for at least a week before you try to put it to use.

When you have a balanced flow of energy, turn your gaze on an object, such as a pencil. Your eyes will act as twin projectors of this energy, filling the object and making it, in its turn, emit energy as well. By first balancing the flow from your eyes, you will make certain that the energy field in the object is given the proper balance of energy and thus assure that it will remain stable. If this is not done, the energy will dissipate as fast as it is put out, and nothing whatever can be expected.

When you have finished loading the object with energy, place your hands over it. You should feel a slight but definite warmth coming from the object. If you move your hands slowly over the object, you should feel the same breeze effect that you felt as you moved your hands over each other.

Now you are ready to build your first, simple device. Take a piece of flat cardboard. Push a pin or needle into it so that when the cardboard is laid, the needle will stand upright. It will not hurt to place a small drop of glue at the point where the needle comes through the cardboard to make certain that it does not wobble, or worse, get squashed. Now take a drinking straw. At the center of the straw make a hole, but be careful that the hole is only on one side of the straw so that the needle does not penetrate the other side. The hole should be large enough so that the straw can turn with virtually no friction. Balance the needle and straw so that the straw is resting on the needle but not touching the cardboard. Place this device where it will not be in any breeze or draft. If you have a bell jar that can cover it so much the better, but it is not necessary to go through the trouble and the expense of finding one. As long as there is no external pressure on the straw everything will be just fine.

Place yourself before the device and sit. Do not stare at it yet. When the straw is still, place either hand over it but be very careful not to touch it. If the straw is touched, it will slip out of balance and you will have to reset the whole thing. Be careful to avoid setting up an air current. When your hand is placed over the straw, it should begin to turn on the needle, either towards the hand or away from it. Remove your hand and let the straw stop. Repeat the procedure with the other hand. In most cases the straw will be attracted by one hand and repelled by the other.

It is now time to find out what your eyes can do. When the straw is motionless, sit comfortably and stare at it, willing the energy to come forth from your eyes and make it turn. The straw should begin to move, usually going so far in one direction and then reversing itself. Some individuals are able to make the device turn completely on its axis, but that is not necessary.

This simple machine is basically a confidence builder. It proves to the person using it that they do have power and can put it to work. It is sometimes not even necessary for a person to have undergone any training in order to achieve results with this device. As an experiment, I asked my mother, who is the greatest skeptic in the known world, to just look at it. She did and it turned for her just as it did for me. Needless to say, she was amazed and to this day is trying to find a "rational" explanation.

What has happened here? You remember my short description of Robert Pavlita's generators. Well, you have just built a cheap version of one, and have done much the same thing that he does in pushing your etheric body out from yourself to cause a physical object to move. This is the much-discussed phenomenon known as psychokinesis. You have just proven it to yourself with a device costing pennies at most, and as most homes have the materials just laying around collecting dust, it may very well have cost literally nothing but the few minutes spent making it.

Having proved to you that you can get results, it is now time for you to progress to better and more interesting things. I am sure that you have heard that if you stare at the back of a person and *will* him to turn, most of the time he will. That is a nice exercise, but let us be honest and admit that merely making a person turn around and look at you is not only a bit boring, it can be downright embarrassing if he should decide to stare back. By means of your power of visualization, you are going to do something which is much more fun, quite harmless, and useful as a means of training your powers so that they will become even greater.

Go to a lecture. I realize that this is a terrible thing to ask, but bear with me. When you enter the hall, sit towards the rear of the audience, so that you will be looking directly at the back of some other person in attendance. As in the usual form, fix your gaze on the back of this person, about the level of the neck, but do not will him to turn around. Instead, see your energy field form itself into a drill and let it bore into the person's neck. He should find that he has some difficulty keeping his mind on the lecture.*

You may experience some difficulty in visualizing with your eyes open. If you do, do not give up hope and consider your work a failure. Repeat the experiment, and simply try to persuade yourself that the drill is there even though you cannot actually see it. This is not as hard as it may seem.

Read a work of fiction, the more descriptive the better. As you read the story, you will notice that in your mind you will see what is happening; that is to say, you will have the same information present in your mind as you would have if your eyes actually saw it, and, as your brain cannot really tell the difference

---

* See Appendix on page 195.

between the two, it will respond as *if* you saw it. The same principle is at work here. You may not actually *see* the drill; very few of us have the talent. But you *can* make your mind work in such a way that it will function as if you did see it. The end result will be much the same.

After you have achieved some degree of success at making people respond to your eye transmissions, you can begin to send simple messages. Some writers on this subject say that you should send out an image of what you wish the recipient to do. While this method will work very well, it is difficult to practice in any social situation unless you have been practicing for some years, and I doubt that you wish to wait that long. I know that I certainly would not. A far easier method is to break down your command until you can express it in one word, such as "Turn!" or "Run!" or, if you have a sense of humor like mine, "Trip!"

Practice this at home, before you try it on anyone. Stand or sit in front of a mirror and stare at yourself. Try to see your etheric body glowing, and, if you cannot do that, implant the knowledge in your mind that it is there and radiating energy. While you are doing this, stare yourself in the eyes. You should notice some strange feelings, but ignore them. They are only the brain responding to the limited information such a stare will send it. Send energy out from *your* eyes into the eyes in the mirror. Remember that the energy can be reflected! You should notice a change of feeling of some kind, but as everyone reacts differently, it is impossible to say exactly what you will feel. It will, however, be different from what you experienced when you simply stared at the mirror.

After you have done this exercise, go out into a crowd and pick a victim; any victim will do provided he or she doesn't seem to be too distracted, such as being actively involved in a conversation. Fix your gaze on the person, preferably from the rear. Admittedly, if you can look directly into the eyes it works better, but there are some very strong social conventions against that sort of thing, so I would advise you to stick to shooting in the back.

Decide on your command. Fix your gaze and send out energy, feeling the stuff of your etheric body expand and flare out from your eyes to extend in a long thin line to the target. Again, you do not actually have to see this, merely know that it is happening. You may even feel the energy leave you, just as Jesus is said to have felt the energy leave him when the woman touched the hem of his garment. In any event, the person should respond to your sending by doing what you wish, but sometimes he will fail to do so. If that is the case, do not give up; pick another victim and blast away again. Remember the old SWAT team motto: "If you keep shooting, you're bound to hit somebody."

By this point, I hope you have figured out how this whole teaching system works. Each exercise is designed to train you for the next one with experiments in between to illustrate the powers, and at the same time give you the confidence to go on or show you that you need to work some more. It cannot be mentioned too often that the two qualities needed most in the psychic field are patience and confidence. If you lack patience, you will become quickly discouraged, like my mother who takes medicine one time, and if she does not get well immediately, is convinced that it does not work. Psychic power works, but you must be willing to *let* it work.

I will now show you a more practical use for this latest ability you have gained. Let us say that you are at a party and you are having a thoroughly miserable time because you came alone and are likely to leave that way. Across the room is a genuinely gorgeous member of the opposite sex and you would sell your grandmother to meet that person. Fortunately, nothing so drastic is required. Get away from the general conversation for a few seconds, because if the party is well-managed, a few seconds may be all you have, and begin to fill yourself with energy. Feel your etheric body expand and contract with your chest as you breathe. Know in your mind that it is beginning to glow, and feel that if all the lights were to suddenly go out in the room you would literally shine. Fix your gaze on the subject, trying to catch his or her eye if possible, and then transmit. As you send out your energy, exhale. It is well-known that the act of exhalation increases the strength of muscles, which is the reason behind the famous Karate yell. The same principle applies here, but do not yell, or you will produce the opposite results of what you wish. By exhaling as you send, you will increase the power of the transmission and improve your chances of success.

After you have gotten the person's attention, choose your word of command. Remember, keep it down to one word. It is best to have chosen this word in advance because you may have to act quickly. Stare at the person for a couple of seconds. You can probably get away with that in a social context at a distance. While staring, shoot your beam directly into those eyes with your command, and then approach the person. You may, if the circumstances are right, not even have to do that. The person may approach you.

Now comes the hard part. After you approach your subject, do not do anything more with your psychic energy until you are certain that you really want to know more about this person. It may be the case that you will meet someone and discover an instant mutual distaste, so it is a good idea to remember that one of the most important things about power is knowing when *not* to use it. Otherwise, you may find yourself getting into more difficulties than you had before. Believe me, I know.

This power can also be used to bring you more wealth and prosperity than you have known before.

By now I can hear some of my readers saying, somewhat unpleasantly, "But I'm happily married and I don't need to find romance." Or worse, "I've got four girlfriends now. The last thing I need is another one." Well, everyone wants more of the green stuff without which life is, after all, hardly worth the trouble of living. Money may be the root of all evil, but the evil that money is the root of is nothing but goodness incarnate when compared to evils that come from the lack of it. Let us be honest. More sleep is lost and more dinners ruined by worry about money than from any other cause. Columbus, when he presented his somewhat novel ideas to the Spanish Court, said "Gold is most excellent. With gold all things may be obtained."

The first prerequisite to using psychic power to bring money to yourself is nothing more than plain, old-fashioned greed. Are you sufficiently shocked? Well, stop feeling that way. If it were not for greed, no human progress would ever occur. It is the motive of wishing for wealth that moves men to take chances, to improve their lot in life. You cannot obtain what you want out of living what you do not first desire, and you must desire it in as positive a way as possible. Now, by positive, I do not mean gushy, sentimental nonsense about helping humanity. The greatest fortunes have been made by men whose only desire to aid humanity was over the nearest cliff. No, by positive, I mean that you truly desire wealth without that desire being polluted by worry.

There you go thinking again. You did not know it was so loud did you? You are thinking "But I'm really worried about this. If I don't pay my brother back the thousand I owe him he'll sell my daughter into white slavery!" Did you ever stop to think what happens when you worry like that? You are setting up a very powerful thought-form which is doing nothing but preventing you from getting money.

Let me explain like this. Before the great market crash of 1929, there was tremendous economic activity. People were employed, goods were produced and purchased. The same physical facilities that were present before the crash were there after it. The only problem lay in the minds of people who did not believe that they were there. They were literally paralyzed by their own fears, and that was why Franklin Roosevelt made his famous comment, so puzzling today after fifty years, that the only thing to fear was fear itself. The same principle applies when you worry about money. In order to be rich, you must first think of yourself as being rich.

Look around you and total up your assets. You have your health, and no, sniffles do not count against it. As long as one part of you functions, that part is an asset, so stop whining. You have this book, which is a very valuable piece of merchandise because you are learning from it. Your very capacity to learn is an asset. No matter how poor you think yourself, you live in greater comfort than kings did a couple of centuries ago. Louis XIV, the Sun King, would have given half his kingdom for an air conditioner. When you are able to look past your immediate circumstances, you will realize that you have quite a bit and are, to begin with, rich.

Every night, before you go to bed, silently or aloud, catalogue those things which you possess that you would count as wealth. Every time you do that, you will help to program your mind to think in terms of being rich. Remember: wealth attracts wealth. The rich get richer because they think that way. The moment you change your thought pattern, you will begin to change your relationship, not only with the visible world but also with the invisible. You will, in your mind, become a wealthy individual and soon you will become such in reality.

So much for step one. As soon as you begin to feel your attitude start to change, you should begin to meditate on the subject of wealth. In the course of your meditations, imagine yourself with those material possessions which you desire. See yourself driving the new car, living in the big house. This act of imagining is very important, not only because it creates a pattern of thought in yourself which will ultimately bring those things to you, but it transforms money from an abstract concept which it really is, to material reality. One of the most difficult problems faced by those who try to use psychic power to bring them money is that they tend to think in terms of figures in a ledger book, rather than in terms of ultimate results.

You can also program your etheric body to bring riches into your life. As you meditate, see the light coming into your body take on a gold or green color. Now this piece of advice will give at least one clairvoyant I know fits, because there are certain beliefs concerning the color of the aura. Do not worry about anything you may have heard or will hear in this regard. Gold and green are colors which our culture associates with wealth and its monetary manifestation, so those are the colors you must use.

See the colored light fill your body, bringing with it the capacity to make money come seemingly out of air. Know that as you fill yourself with the light, your etheric body is being charged to attract money to you. Perform this exercise every day without fail until you begin to see results. They may not be spectacular at first. It may only be finding a dollar on the street, but it will be something that will let you gain the confidence to go on.

As you continue to charge your etheric body to attract money to you, you should also notice that you begin to have hunches that pay off. This is not to suggest that you go to a race track and put all your money down on a long shot because your hunch told you to. You must also use a little sense in this. What you *should* get are definite ideas on how to make money. You may dream of a certain person who is going to hire you. If you do, go and ask for a job. The worst thing that can happen is that you may be turned down. If that occurs, do not be discouraged. Keep trying. Test your intuitions, and soon you will learn that they can be quite accurate.

When you do go for a job or try to sell something, you must prepare for it. You should imagine yourself talking to the person whom you wish to impress, and at the same time clearly imagine him being interested and buying. Build this image up as strongly as you can before you even walk into the room. Your etheric body can also be used. Before you go to see the person, meditate on the energy filling your etheric body. Command it to fill you and remain stored until it is needed. When that time comes, send the energy from your eyes, just like the beams from two car headlights. It is not necessary to actually see this energy stream forth, but you should be strongly convinced that it is doing so. Imagine, as clearly and powerfully as possible, that these beams are burning into the soul of your target, driving the message you wish to send into his brain like a heated nail. With enough practice, you should be able to do this almost instantaneously. You are working with the speed of thought, so it is not necessary to transmit for long periods of time. In point of fact, this sort of thing is best done when done quickly, like a kind of psychic guerilla raid.

There is a reason why prolonged use of a burning

gaze can be counter-productive. It works best without blinking, and, in our Western culture, people react very strongly and usually unpleasantly to being stared at in business. It makes them nervous and then hostile. We want to avoid that, so keep it short.

Sometimes you may be lucky enough to have met the person you are going to deal with before you contact him about your latest proposal. If that is the case, you can soften him up with a preliminary bombardment. I meant that quite literally. You are going to use psychic power in exactly the same way as an army uses its heavy artillery. You are going to stand off and blast him from a distance before moving in for the final assault.

Again, you sit and meditate. Relax yourself as best you can, and by now that should be fairly easy. Do not doubt that your sendings are going to reach the subject, but continue to transmit, knowing as surely as you can that you are getting into his consciousness.

"Very nice," you are thinking, "but what do I send?"

Rule one: Do not send a command. You want this person to like both you and your ideas. Commands sometimes have the unfortunate tendency to backfire if they should hit at the wrong moment. This is not to say that they should not be used or that they do not work, but if you want to be sure, it is best to couch your sendings with thoughts which are soothing, and, if possible, complimentary.

Rule two: Unlike the meeting situation, where it is necessary to act as quickly as possible, you should take your time about this, and send as often as you can for as long as you can.

As you meditate, try to visualize the person you are trying to contact. See him as a happy, receptive individual who is only too happy to meet you again and listen to your pitch. Think that you will be equally pleased to renew the acquaintance, and send your thoughts in such a way as to convey this. Incidentally, this is a good way to smooth over those little embarrassments which befall us from time to time. If you have somehow managed to make a fool of yourself, simply think at the person you have managed to offend how much you like him or her, and you will be amazed at the results. I must confess to being more than a little outspoken, and this method has saved my skin many a time.

As you are mentally telling this individual how much you like him and even how much you like working for him or with him, picture him as responding in the same way to you. If you have enough time to do this, you should have a well-softened person to do business with by the time you meet him.

Now for a word of warning. There are times when, in spite of our best efforts, the results are not quite what we would desire. It is absolutely essential that you not feel defeated by such failures. Much as we would like to pretend otherwise, no system is foolproof, and it may be that you have wasted a tremendous amount of time sending good thoughts to a fool (pearls before swine, as it were). Or, it may be that what you have to sell really does not meet his needs, such as air conditioning for Antarctica. You must never interpret a less than positive response as any failure on your own part, at least as far as your use of psychic power is concerned.

This brings us to one of the most powerful psychic weapons you can put in your arsenal—the stationary thought-form, or as it is sometimes called, the Psychic Land Mine.

It is possible to use your psychic power to charge any place or anything with enough energy to influence those who pass by it. There are even those few lucky individuals who can even make visible forms out of virtual thin air, but we are not even going to try that.

You have already learned how to create a small thought-form and send it on its way to a target. Now, you are going to do much the same thing, but, instead of hitting a given individual, you are going to have it affect the mind of everyone who passes near it. It is a very simple process, and one which is well worth learning.

Back to the lecture hall. Let us assume you are going to speak on some arcane subject, such as the art and mystery of naked options. You are reasonably certain that everyone who comes to hear you will be at least slightly interested in your topic, but, as you are going to approach it from a slightly unconventional point of view, you are not sure how well your talk is going to be received. For this, there is a simple and sure method.

You should have a good idea of the general physical appearance of the hall you are going to speak in. If possible, view it in advance. It will make working with your thought-form that much easier.

You create your thought-form by the usual method,

but this time, you place it in the center of the room, up near the ceiling like a lamp. In fact, if you can visualize it as a lamp, so much the better. See it glow with light and take the energy that makes it glow out of the air, that energy being the very driving stuff of the universe. Charge it to make everyone who is bathed by that light receptive to you and to your ideas. See the lamp illuminate the entire hall, leaving no place in the shadows. Continue to charge the lamp and do so as often as possible, always reminding it that anyone who is touched by the beam will respond positively to you.

What happens then? On the day for the lecture, the audience comes into the hall and sits down, not realizing that their individual minds are being manipulated in your favor. As the beams from the lamp play over their psychic bodies, they will find themselves liking you and what you have to say without even questioning why.

You may also use this on an individual level. You wish to impress a certain idea on a given individual; let us call him Person A. You have already tried the other methods I have given you and had no results, which may happen. You have an idea of what his office looks like, so you begin meditating. You see in your mind that office. You do not have to be too detailed, just enough so that you know what you are looking at. Now, you create your thought-form, but instead of sending it directly at the individual in question, you send it to that office, placing it over the door so that anyone walking in will be influenced by it. You impregnate the thought-form with your message and let it work. If you remember to send a charge to it each time you meditate, you should notice some results.

This method can also be used to protect your property and eliminate nuisances. Let me give you an example. A neighbor of ours had the annoying habit of walking his dog down the alley, and the dog had taken a liking to our garbage cans. Needless to say, this was a serious matter, made even more difficult by the fact that this neighbor was an otherwise nice person whom we did not wish to offend. I created a thought-form which would have no other effect than to make the dog do his business elsewhere, and it worked. The dog refused to stop in his usual spot, and the puzzled neighbor had to lead the noble beast all around the block before he found a new one.

It can serve the same function with humans. If your neighborhood should suddenly find itself beset by burglars, it is but a simple matter to create a thought-form which will bar them from your property. Simply create the form, set it in the air over the center of your home, and charge it so that it bathes your property with its protective rays.

There are myriad other uses for these excellent instruments, the number and type being bounded only by imagination. The basic rules for their use are easy to remember.

1) You must be certain that you want the results that you are programming for.

2) You must keep the commands as simple as possible.

3) You must always phrase the command in a positive way, never using a negative in the statement of purpose.

4) You must remember to keep charging the thought-forms as long as you wish them to operate.

Now all this may have the appearance of a complicated psychological game. If you believe that something is going to happen for you, you will act in such a way as to make it happen. That is all very good as an argument, but you should take into account the fact that even if you act on the assumption that you will attain your ends, that is no guarantee of the fact that somebody else may work for your ends. There is more to this than extended auto-suggestion.

Never forget that we are dealing here with energies that are quite real, have significant evidence to prove their reality, and are quite capable of causing effects at enormous distances. What is more, I am now going to teach you how to build simple versions of machines that are now available which have been proven to detect and manipulate these energies.

3

The Pendulum

Now that you have mastered the control of your etheric body, and have discovered the wonderful use to which that body can be put, we can move on to some of the devices themselves. In doing so we are going to be studying psionics proper, and we begin with that aspect of it which is called dowsing, or Radiesthesia, which is a word that I hate because it sounds like something found in hospitals.

Dowsing is something that has been around for a very long time—in fact so long that we cannot begin to put a date on it. It has been used to find water, minerals and even land mines. It is the simplest of all psionic activities, calling for the easiest devices, many of them harkening back to the Stone Age. The picture of the rustic with his forked stick has become something of a comic figure, but it was a very serious business when there was no other way of finding out if a particular spot was a good place to dig a well. There are some very interesting old drawings of German miners in the fifteenth and sixteenth centuries going around with the same stocks trying to discover hidden metals.*

---

*Grillot De Givry, *The Illustrated Anthology of Sorcery, Magic and Alchemy*, Trans. by J. Courtenay Locke (New York: Causeway Books, 1973) pp. 312-313.

We, however, are not going to waste our time with forked sticks. They are a bit cumbersome to carry around, and I have never had much luck with them anyway. There is a much better instrument available that you can easily make, and that is the old, reliable pendulum.

I have never ceased to be amazed at how people react to the idea of using a pendulum as a psychic instrument. To judge by their first reactions, you would think I was suggesting that they carry an old grandfather clock around with them. Nothing could be further from the truth. In point of fact, many people, including myself, have written about the pendulum and there are a number of varieties on the market. I have used one myself for many years now, and I will try to make both the device and its use as simple as possible for you.

To begin with, a working pendulum can be any weight attached to a string. Some authors go into great detail on what type of weight should be used, some saying it can be as simple as a ring (which is, incidentally, a very bad thing to use), others trying to sell more complicated devices fitted with magnets, or hollow, or made out of Juju wood, or something. In my own experience, I have found that a simple, cheap child's top makes an excellent pendulum. They are still relatively easy to find and usually quite inexpensive. They even come with their own string! You should never forget that psychic power in all its manifestations is one of the few genuine bargains left in the world, and you should never spend good money on an instrument if you can make it yourself. In fact, if you make the instrument yourself, you can be absolutely certain that the device is uncontaminated by the thought impressions of anyone else, something that you cannot be sure of with a commercial device.

Once you have bought the top, drill a hole into the center of the flat top and insert a small screw eye. After you have accomplished this small feat, attach the string to the screw eye (*see figure 1*). Since the string which comes with the top will most likely be too long for convenience, determine which length is best for you. This will usually be between twelve and eighteen inches. Cut the string to the desired length and tie a small knot at the end to make holding easier.

The pendulum itself has four basic movements. It will swing back and forth away from you, from left to

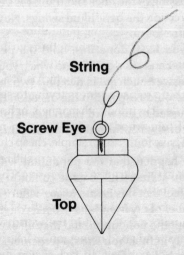

Figure 1

right, or it may circle either clockwise or counter-clockwise. It may also just jiggle in no pattern at all. The jiggle usually occurs only when you are holding the pendulum and asking it no particular question, and is the result of small unconscious movements of your hand. Other than that, the swings of the pendulum have their own meanings. In most cases, when it swings forward and back away from you it is signifying a positive response. If it is moving from left to right it is a negative answer, and circling means that it does not know. At times this may vary with individuals, and some have discovered that when it circles clockwise it means yes and counterclockwise means no. You may have to experiment to find out. Make a copy of figure 2 and lay it on a table in front of you. Hold the pendulum over the crossing of the lines and think yes very hard. Note the direction the pendulum swings. Now repeat the procedure for no.

Once you have done this, hold the pendulum over the center and ask a question to which you already know the answer, such as "Is two plus two four? The pendulum should respond to the question the same way it responded to the word yes. If it does not, something is wrong with the question, or you are not concentrating.

It may happen that the pendulum will barely move for you at first. This is quite common and you should not feel that this is due to any failure on your part. A number of my friends have been convinced by me to attempt the pendulum, and they all experience *some* difficulty at first. You should remember that the ability to use any instrument comes from practice, and

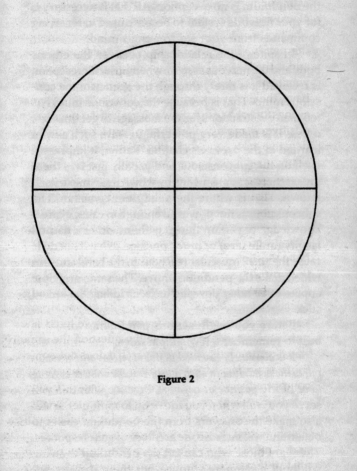

Figure 2

the pendulum is no exception. All that is necessary is for your nervous system to become used to receiving commands from your subconscious mind.

In spite of the relationship between the etheric body and the nervous system, when a psychic reception is received it is rarely through the agency of the conscious mind. That is because the conscious mind has too many distractions for the message to get through, unless it is made very powerful in ways such as you learned in the previous chapter. Rather, it impresses itself on the subconscious and usually just lays there unless there is some means by which it can make itself known. That is where the pendulum comes in. The subconscious is not powerful enough to cause a direct knowledge of certain things without either a natural faculty (quite rare) or much practice. What it *can* do is cause the small muscular reactions in the hand and arm which make the pendulum move. The same principle applies to all other dowsing tools, including the forked stick.

Before you begin serious pendulum work, it is best to remember a few simple rules.

It is absolutely essential that you phrase any question put to the pendulum in such a way that the answer is going to be clearly positive or negative. Practice with this will serve you well when you move on to radionics. It will also make the answers from the pendulum easier to obtain and will increase the accuracy of your responses. There are those who can get the pendulum to swing wildly at a moment's notice but their answers are always wrong.

The pendulum will only give answers to questions on

which it has information. There will be times when it gives no answer because the information is not present. This is not due to any failing on your part.

Your conscious mind can control the pendulum. You should never ask it a question about which you have a strong emotional response, because if you do the pendulum will only tell you what you wish to hear.

So much for the warnings. Now let us get on to the uses for this wonderful little device.

Telling Time

One of the more entertaining, albeit somewhat frivolous, uses to which the pendulum has been put is to tell time. When the pendulum became popular among psychic experimenters about a century ago, this faculty caused a tremendous stir. They would get up in the middle of the night, and in the dark, hold the pendulum near a wall and ask what the hour was. They found their tests inevitably yielded positive results; so positive, in fact, that a number of them forgot to wind their clocks.

You may duplicate the experiments yourself. Hold the pendulum next to a wall, or even a piece of furniture. Then simply ask it to tell you what time it is. The pendulum will begin to swing, slowly at first and then with more speed until it strikes the wall. It will then measure itself, striking the wall only that number of times which is the equal of the hour. So, if you ask it to tell you the time at three, it will knock three times and then stop swinging. If it is asked the time on the half-hour, it will strike loudly the number of the hour and then strike once, softly, to signify the half. Now in case you are wondering what use this ability can be, I would have you think back to the last time you were waiting for the arrival, usually late, of a delivery or a repair person. You were stuck in the house because you did not wish to miss the doorbell. With the pendulum, you will be able to avoid that problem. All you have to do is ask when the washing machine fixer is going to arrive. It will tell you the hour, and you can relax until then. If he does not come at the appointed time, you should not blame the pendulum. It can only give you information which was available at the time you asked. Thus, if you ask at nine in the morning, the pendulum will give you the answer which applied at the time. But the washing machine fixer may encounter a problem which took longer than he realized, and force him to delay getting to you. If you ask the pendulum again, it will give you a more accurate arrival time. When I use the pendulum for this purpose, I make a point of asking it at least once an hour, and in that way I am rarely disappointed.

Finding Lost Objects

But by far the most common and effective use of the pendulum is the finding of lost objects. In this way, the pendulum acts as the traditional divining instrument that it is. Let us assume that you have a lost object of value somewhere in your house; let us say a diamond ring. Now a diamond is not something you would like to lose. You want it found and fast, but you have no idea of where to look. Despair not, for you have your trusty pendulum. Stand and hold the pendulum out away from you while visualizing the ring. The pendulum will begin to swing in the direction of the lost object.

All you have to do is follow it until the pendulum begins to swing in a circle or stops altogether. The lost ring should be at that point.

I have used this technique a number of times and it has never failed to amaze those who were with me. Let me give an example.

When I was young and in school, I worked during the summer for my father who ran a screw-machine shop. The machines were old models, and because of their advanced years, had a tendency to fall apart, sometimes a little dramatically. This happened one morning when a gadget called the stock-bar feed, which was placed at one end of the machine, came loose and sent a part flying off into orbit, or so it seemed. All work stopped, and we looked high and low for the missing piece. The shop was busy and the machine could not be left idle, so we crawled around in the oil vainly searching for the missing part. But, no matter where we looked, the part was nowhere to be found. Things were getting pretty desparate at Acco Engineering that morning. Father was beginning to run out of swear words when I remembered the pendulum. Actually, it did not take much remembering because I was just starting to experiment with it and could hardly resist the chance to use it. It might have looked a little foolish, but being the boss' son has some advantages, and no one else was having any luck. So I made a quick, makeshift device with a cam and some twine, and asked it where the missing part was. It pointed to the general direction that we had been looking in and for a moment I felt really stupid, because we had been over that area so much that not a bolt had been undiscovered. In fact, we found a whole bunch of lost items, but no part. But I did not give up. I followed the pendulum until it stopped over a barrel which contained a substance called oil-dry, which is similar in composition to kitty-litter and was used to dry up oil spilled on the floor. The barrel had an open top and the part had flown off the machine, into the barrel and had managed to bury itself under several inches of the stuff.

There is also another method of finding things with a pendulum and it is very effective. Let us say that you are out of doors, in a large field and you have somehow lost your favorite golf ball. The field is too big for you to simply follow the pendulum, so you take a reading, holding the pendulum and noting which direction it swings. Having done that, walk some distance from where you took your first reading and ask the pendulum again. Again, note the direction taken by the pendulum. Where the lines cross, that is where you should find the missing ball; at least in the vicinity. It is then a good idea to take the pendulum to that spot and ask it again where the ball is. This time, it should lead you directly to it.

Map Dowsing

A similar use for the pendulum involves a practice known as map dowsing. This is a time-honored method of finding such things as water and minerals, and some talented individuals have even shopped for a home using this method. It is very simple, but can be a little time consuming. Let us assume that you own a large tract of land, such as a cattle ranch, and due to a depressed market, do not wish to spend money for a water survey without having some idea of where to look first. If the ranch is big enough, there will be a map somewhere detailing it. Take this map and hold the pendulum at one side and ask it to find the spot for the well. Note the direction the pendulum swings. Repeat the procedure at the other side of the map. Where the lines cross, you should find your water.

If you are looking for something on a large map, such as the ideal town to move to, begin by holding the pendulum over the vertical coordinates of the map, moving the pendulum along the edge of the map until it begins to swing. Note that spot and repeat the process along the horizontal coordinates until you get a similar response. The intersection of those two co-ordinates will be the place you are looking for.

This is not so far-fetched as it seems. The technique

of map dowsing has a number of highly beneficial uses.

For example, lost people can be found relatively easily by this method, where more conventional search methods would take far too long. Some friends of mine were out camping a few years ago and their child wandered off into the woods. Being friends of mine, they were thoroughly indoctrinated in the use of the pendulum. In fact, I'm afraid I may have bored them with my lecturing. Fortunately, they remembered what I had taught them and happened to have with them a geological survey map which covered literally every crook and gully of the area they were in. The father took out his pendulum, went over the edges of the map as I have described and was able to find the child within a hundred yards of the spot the pendulum told him to look. By the time the forest rangers, summoned by the frantic mother, had arrived, father and son were back at the camp site.

Lie Detector

You can use the pendulum in such a manner as to make certain that you are never deceived again. For some years now, there have been machines available which can make a determination as to the truthfulness of a person by analyzing stress patterns in the voice. The pendulum can fulfill the same role with a much higher degree of accuracy for the simple reason that the user of the pendulum is measuring not the muscular stress on the vocal chords of the speaker, but rather the psychic stress which comes from the telling of a deliberate untruth, and, in the hands of a sufficiently

The Pendulum / 63

skilled operator, can even detect an inadvertent lie. In other words, the person may *think* he is telling the truth based on the information he has available, but in fact he is not, simply because he was given the wrong information.

You begin by turning on the television some evening when the news is on and placing your copy of figure 2 in front of you. When some spokesman comes on whose job it is to try to explain the latest disaster, hold the pendulum over the center of the circle and ask it to tell you if the truth is being told. It will swing in the appropriate direction. Or, you can simply instruct the pendulum to tell you if a lie is being told, and how bad a lie it is. As soon as that occurs, the pendulum will begin to swing. In the case of a minor fib, it will move only slightly, but if the statement is a genuine whopper, the swing may be quite extreme. I tried this during the last election campaign, and several times the pendulum swung so hard that it actually looped itself over my hand.

If you are talking to somebody, you may not want to have the pendulum hanging from your fingers at that time. After all, we do not want to be thought of as being completely out of our minds. When you get home hold the pendulum over the circle while concentrating on the person with whom you had the conversation, and ask the pendulum if he was telling the truth. The pendulum will tell you, but there is one very important thing that you must be careful of when you use the pendulum for this purpose. The pendulum can be made to give you the answer that you *wish* it to give, so if you feel strongly one way or the other about the answer, you had best not use the pendulum because it will give you the response you expect rather than the one which is true. When you use the pendulum to gain any type of information, it is best to cultivate an attitude of disinterest about that piece of information. This may not always be possible, but it is the best way to assure accuracy.

For example, a close friend of mine had something stolen from her and she knew, beyond any possible doubt, that it was stolen by a fellow worker. Now there was no evidence to indicate who the thief might be, and she was far too upset to use the pendulum with any degree of accuracy. I offered to use it for her, being of a generous nature. I told her to make a list of everyone with whom she worked. I laid it in front of me. I then held the pendulum in my right hand and moved my left index finger down the list, stopping for about ten seconds at each name, mentally commanding the pendulum to tell me who the culprit was. It remained motionless until it arrived at one name and then began to circle. I noted that and continued down until I had asked about every name. Then I went back and asked the pendulum if the person it had picked was the thief. It swung in a strong, positive response. The swing of a pendulum is, however, hardly sufficient evidence to back a serious accusation, at least in the mind of my friend, but she was at least careful not to trust this particular individual with anything in the future.

Help in Relationships

The pendulum can give you a great deal of useful information in the area of romance, but you must be able to keep an open mind, or the only response you will get will be positive, even if the truth is negative. Never ask the pendulum anything if you are enamored, but if the relationship is just starting and you are not sure if you should pursue it, the pendulum can be of great assistance.

For this purpose it is good to have a photograph of the other person. It can also work if you just write the person's name on a piece of paper, but a photograph works best, particularly for a beginner.

Lay the picture in front of you on a table and hold the pendulum over the face of the person. It is not necessary to ask the pendulum to do anything. If the individual in the photograph likes you, the pendulum will register positive and if the contrary is the case, the pendulum will register negative. A person who knows how to use a pendulum can save himself much grief by asking it the right questions about anyone he or she is involved with. But I have to repeat the warning that if you are already emotionally committed, the pendulum will do nothing more than to confirm your suspicions or desires.

The Pendulum Can Act as a Gauge to Test the Effectiveness of Your Thought-forms.

In the previous chapter you learned how to create and use thought-forms. The pendulum can be used to tell you if they have successfully reached their target. Before you create your thought-form, write the name you have assigned to the thought-form, if you have named it, or the nature of the command you have given it down on a piece of paper and keep that in a safe place. Send out your thought-form and forget it for a day or two. After that time has elapsed, when you have a free moment, take out the paper and ask the pendulum if the thought-form has accomplished its purpose. If it gives you a positive response, there is no need for further action. But if the response is negative, you can create a new thought-form to replace the old one or you can reinforce the existing thought-form by meditation, sending more energy to it, feeding it. If you are in doubt as to which method is best, you can ask the pendulum to advise you.

The Pendulum Can Be Used to Trace the Etheric Body.

Let us return to the basic make-up of the human body. You will remember I told you that in addition to the physical body, there is coexistent with it the etheric body, and everything which takes place in the physical has its counterpart in the etheric. Now we are forced to admit that we have no idea of what the etheric body is made of. There is a common belief that it is in some way electrical, and this has been reinforced by the research which has been done using Kirlian photography. But, as we have seen in our study, this etheric body and the stuff that makes it can do things which electricity can do. You cannot, for example, make a thought-form out of electricity, though electrical conductors can be used to carry a thought-form to its target, even though that technique is highly inefficient. This simple fact being the case, the definition of the energy body as being purely electrical in nature must be considered as incorrect. Unfortunately, that leaves us with a mystery, which, disappointing as it may seem, I am not even going to attempt to solve. It is more than sufficient for our purposes to know that the etheric body exists, and that its existence is detectable by the use of the pendulum. Furthermore, certain aspects of that body can be studied by the use of the pendulum.

One of the more interesting features of the etheric body is that it does not manifest itself equally in all places around the physical body. Rather, it seems to be strongest in places called, for convenience by those who take this sort of thing very seriously, "nodes." It is at these nodes that the energy from the body is most readily detectable, and there is also a correlation between each node and a function of the physical body. When the pendulum comes into contact with one of the nodes it will tend to move much more strongly than it would normally.

You can prove this for yourself. Sit in front of a table and lay your left hand on it. Hold the pendulum over it with your right hand, asking the pendulum to move when it hits one of these nodes. Begin to move the pendulum *slowly* away from your hand. As you do so, you will discover that the pendulum will either only move in certain places or move more strongly at those places. Those are the energy nodes of your hand and if you were to do this around your entire body, you would find yourself with a rather complicated map which would detail the extent of your etheric body. I do not expect you to do this, for at this stage in our study it is more in the nature of an interesting experiment that you may want to try later on.

An Excellent Communication Tool

By means of the pendulum, you can receive messages from any mind you attune to. To do this you will need to make a chart. Get a sheet of paper, the larger the better (within bounds of reason), a drawing compass, and a ruler.

Draw a large circle on the paper. Evenly spaced around the circle, write the letters of the alphabet, from A to Z, numbers 1 through 0, and some common punctuation marks; a period and comma should suffice. Take the ruler and draw a line from the center of the circle to a point between each letter, number and mark. This will give you a circle divided into narrow wedges. If you wish, you may color each wedge, but if you do, be absolutely certain that no segment is colored the same as the one on either side. This is very important, and if you do it wrong you will have to start over. When you have finished, the sheet, combined with your pendulum, is your receiver.

So how does it work? Let us say that you want to know what your spouse is planning for supper. This is a good thing to start with as it is easily verified. Begin by meditating for a short period. This will help clear your mind of the usual extraneous garbage that some-times manages to come through while using this arrangement. Hold the pendulum over the center of the circle and think about your question. The pendulum will begin to move along one of the wedges toward a letter. At first, the swing may be erratic, and you may have some trouble deciding which letter it is aiming for, but quickly the pendulum will settle down, and the first letter of the answer will be obvious. At that point stop the pendulum and bring it back to the center. As soon as it stops, let it begin to point out the next letter and continue the procedure until you have the complete message. At that point, the pendulum will stop over the center and hang motionless.

The uses of this simple device should be obvious. If one of your thought-forms is not working, the pendulum, which is in better touch with your subconscious than you are, can tell you why it is not, and even tell you how to correct the problem. But there is the usual difficulty in this.

The pendulum, as I have said before, can be so influenced by the conscious mind that it will only tell you what you may wish to hear. You may greatly desire a particular result and send out a series of thought-forms to attain it, but you are still disappointed with the results. The pendulum may tell you that you are well on the road to getting what you want when you may be as far from it as ever. At that point, the pendulum has become, rather than a tool, a cheering section. Because of this, it is very important to use discretion in what you ask, and never ask the pendulum to merely confirm a suspicion.

And with that we end our study of the pendulum. Now, on to Radionics.

4

Radionics

Okay, gang, now that we have finished with our good friend the pendulum, we can get down to the part that you have all been waiting for—Radionics. Of all the many aspects and techniques involved in psychic power, none has been more controversial. And this is not without good reason. The idea that it is possible to significantly affect people and even influence their thoughts by turning dials on a box with, in most modern cases, no power other than the mind of the operator at work is hardly the stuff from which rational decisions are made.

If you find the material that I am about to present a bit hard to swallow, you are certainly not going to be alone. As I mentioned at the beginning of this volume, I first encountered radionics when I was sixteen in a small paperback of the type common back in the mid-sixties. I'm sure you have seen them. Usually written by a writer who made his living turning out one a month, they had covers with drawings on them and little blurbs speaking of the "mysterious box which can see thoughts," or the woman who gave birth to her twenty-first child in a steamer trunk." This was not

71

the environment which would make a believer out of anyone but the most deliriously credulous of individuals and as they all went off and got religion, I was not about to group myself in that category. I read a little of the account in the book of the de la Warr laboratory in England and was immediately convinced that the whole concept was too preposterous to be taken seriously. I was wrong.

Ten years later, I encountered an article about another radionic researcher, T. Galen Hieronymus, which was so written as to make me re-think about my earlier disbelief and try to build a radionic device of my own. To my vast surprise, it worked and has worked for me ever since.

I am going to introduce these machines with a little bit of history. I hope it does not bore you because I find it to be fascinating, and I think after reading it you will, too.

The whole field was created when Dr. Albert Abrams, a doctor in San Francisco (I can hear you muttering, "naturally"), was examining a patient just after the turn of the century. He was percussing a patient, which does not mean that he was swearing, but that he was gently tapping the man's stomach area in the hope of defining the true size of the stomach. It must be remembered that X rays had just been discovered. Abrams, while doing this, received something of a surprise—and also an inspiration. Expecting to hear the usual hollow echo from his tapping, he got a dull note as if there were a solid mass of blubber under the finger. As the man was not fat, the good doctor became curious and felt the area to try and find something under the skin. He found nothing. He repeated the percussion and heard the hollow sound he had expected in the first place. Genuinely puzzled, this man of science asked the patient to walk around the room while he repeated the experiment. The dull note returned. Convinced that he had made one of the rare discoveries which change the world, Dr. Abrams spent the rest of the afternoon moving the patient, who was paying for all this, around the office and tapping his belly. The result of all this labor was the discovery that his patient, who had a cancerous ulcer on his upper lip but no other symptoms, gave a distinct reaction when facing west and only when facing west.

After repeating this experiment on a number of other patients, of which there were many, as Dr. Abrams was by no means the quack he had become to be considered, he came to the conclusion that there was a mysterious force present which caused the particular reacting, and, as he was something of a specialist in the workings of the nervous system, he came to the conclusion (obvious to him) that this force was electrical in nature. In the process of coming to this conclusion, he performed an experiment which would seem to have no electrical basis whatever, but that was not the way it seemed at the turn of the century.

From among his students he selected an assistant who was as healthy a specimen as he could find. He handed the young man a specimen of malignant tumor in a bottle and asked him to face west, holding the bottle to his forehead, while he percussed the student's tummy. He got the expected response and concluded that a piece of diseased tissue, enclosed in a container, could affect the response of a normal person.

Assuming the emanations from the diseased tissue to be electronic in some way (the apparent inconsistency of those radiations passing through an insulating substance notwithstanding), he decided that they could be made to travel down a wire. Let us not pick on Abrams too much. After all, Columbus thought he had found India.

Dr. Abrams acquired two aluminum discs and a six-foot length of wire. One disc was fastened to an insulated handle, and the wire was run to the other disc which was fastened to a subject's forehead with a rubber band. A second assistant stood behind a screen, invisible to Abrams and the subject, and pointed the disc at the ceiling. Abrams percussed the subject and heard the usual, hollow sound. The assistant was then instructed to hold the disc above a cancer specimen without telling the doctor when he was doing so. As soon as the disc was over the specimen, the dull note emerged. Dr. Abrams had proven that this energy could travel down a wire. He also proved that there was a relationship between the energies involved and the electrical activity of the brain.

But our story has just begun. Dr. Abrams was convinced that he could now detect cancer by this somewhat unorthodox method, but suffered what appeared to be a setback when he discovered the same response from syphilis. This presented something of a problem, but Abrams was not a man to be daunted. In the best traditions of early twentieth-century science, he had in his laboratory a three-dial variable resistance box. This was a wooden box with three old-fashioned click rheostats wired in series.

If the story by now is beginning to sound like a 'thirties monster movie, with the mad scientist just happening to have the right materials at hand, I sympathize with you. Certainly much thought and time must have gone into these discoveries, but the accounts simply jump from one to the next, and it is nearly impossible to judge just how difficult the work really was. Suffice it to say that Dr. Abrams was a man of extraordinary insight and was able to come to conclusions which permitted him to continue to develop his ideas and transform them into working apparatus.

Needless to say, his intuition about the use of the resistance box was correct. He wired the box in between the subject whose stomach he was using as a "detector" and the cancer specimen. There was no reaction in the subject, thus proving that the radiations were somehow blocked, but when the assistant turned the dials on the box, the subject eventually reacted.

The importance of this breakthrough cannot be overestimated. The entire concept upon which the use of radionic devices is built is the all-important "rate." The rate is nothing more than the final reading on the dials of a box after the operator has concluded his work with that device.

To explain in a little more detail, the usual radionic instrument has a number of calibrated dials, the numbers usually running from one to ten. As the machine is set, each dial will read a number, and the final rate will be the assemblage of the numbers from each dial; so that if you have a three-dial machine and the final rate is 537, that would mean that the first dial reads 5, the second 3 and the third 7.

Now, all of this was very confusing to Abrams' contemporaries who came to the conclusion that the good doctor had taken leave of his senses. And it must be admitted that Abrams and his followers did little good to their cause by giving strange names to their machines, in what must have been an effort to sound impressive but only attained the opposite results. They were also guilty of over-enthusiasm at times, and that can be certain death for any idea. It must be admitted that the system was far from fool-proof, and there are a certain number of fools who will latch on to anything. Abrams himself, when once trying to demonstrate his skill, proved at a most embarrassing moment to be unable to tell the difference between the blood of a man and a specimen from a rabbit. Hardly the sort of thing which creates great confidence in the more traditional medical community, but a phenomenon which has always bedevilled psychics and psychic research.

But to return to Dr. Abrams. In spite of an occasional attack of overconfidence, he continued to learn the intricacies of his machines. He discovered that a spot of blood from a patient would yield the same results as having the patient wired to the machine. The blood spot was termed the "witness" and this term is now used to describe any sample placed in a radionic device to indicate the target. Now, as you raise your eyebrows at the last statement, you should know that Abrams' next discovery of importance to us is the fact that energy could be sent from the machine to the individual being treated.

Abrams was convinced that there were rates which could neutralize disease, and he directed his efforts to finding them. The outcome of this was a machine called the Oscilloclast. The Oscilloclast was wired to the patient by the means of the same type of electrode he had used in his first experiment years before, and given a peculiar combination of radio-frequency charges and electrical charges. It was apparently successful because about that time Abrams began getting a lot of attention, not all of it favorable.

After Abrams' death, the banner was carried by a number of individuals, most of whom are of little interest to us. Ruth Drown was one, a practitioner who invented the stick plate and got into terrible legal trouble because of the claims made for radionics and healing, which by the 1930's, when she was working, did not seem as reasonable as in Abrams' day; largely because electronics was no longer the mystery it had been. Her work, however, led to the work of George de la Warr in England, who established the Radionic Association, discovered for all practical purposes that radionics is a form of psychic activity and set up a whole spate of ethical guidelines for its practitioners, virtually all of which we will violate in our study.

There is one more researcher who is, at this writing, still working, and that is T. Galen Hieronymus, creator of what is probably the most used radionic device in this country, called, appropriately enough, the Hieronymus Machine. I am not going to go into any great detail about his device. There are many pieces of good literature on the subject available and you can find them with little difficulty. The machine itself, is, for our purposes, a bit on the old-fashioned side, difficult to build, and, while extremely effective, no more effective than the devices I am going to teach you how to make in a little while. The real importance of Hieronymus is the simple fact that, faced with the extreme hostility of the medical profession and its legal guardians to radionics, he had the good sense to not mention healing at all, in either his research or his patent.

Hieronymus, being the cagey fellow that he is, got around the problem of the usual public reactions to radionics by describing his machine as a device for identifying minerals. Now that struck some as odd, because by 1949, there were already some very good conventional tests that could figure out the composition of rocks and such, so why would anyone bother to use the Hieronymus Machine? The answer was obvious to anyone familiar with radionics and the legal problems that have beset it in medical use in this country. While a medical device could come under the scrutiny of the FDA, a machine, even one as unorthodox as this, which was designed to detect minerals, would be untouched.

It was, however, the fact that someone had finally admitted that radionics had a practical use other than in medicine that caught the imagination of experimenters, and ever since there have been any number of radionic devices built for a variety of purposes.

It was discovered about the same time (a little before, in fact) that radionic machines could be used to control insects. Furthermore, they could do it using an aerial photograph of the field to be treated, and it worked so well that the agricultural community rejoiced and the chemical companies had a fit. There was a great deal of fuss and conflicting charges and counter-charges. The pesticide makers carried the day, but the issue is still very much in doubt, and while agricultural radionics does not receive the attention it used to, it is still being practiced, though now by individual farmers rather than by companies.

But enough of this. Before I put you to sleep, I had better start to explain why radionic devices work in the first place.

This, I must warn you, is going to sound a bit complicated and is mostly theory, but, as everyone who has experimented with radionics has their own pet ideas, you might as well hear mine.

A radionic instrument has two functions: tuning and transmitting. In performing both of these it acts directly upon the energy field surrounding a given individual in such a manner as to isolate the different activities or patterns in that field, and either emphasize them or depress them.

Allow me to clarify that statement. The common conception of the human energy field is that of a more or less homogeneous mass of etheric energy. This is not, however, the case. In reality, the etheric body is something more like what you see when you break up light with a prism, the many different wavelengths combining to make the whole. So it is with the etheric body. In working with light, we can use colored filters to isolate a particular wavelength; so it is in working with radionics. By using the machines we can isolate bands of energy in the etheric body. By means of this isolation, we can discover many useful things. For example, a man stubs his toe. He feels the pain of the toe, anger at himself for having stubbed it in the first place, and the physical reaction in the toe itself upsets him because it gets slightly swollen. All the while the nerve endings in the toe are shouting *pain* and that is what caused all the other reactions in the first place. These all show up in the etheric body, and by means of properly tuned radionic devices we can isolate each reaction.

We are able to isolate these waves because they show up in the etheric body. The term for them is "wave-form." Some psychics would consider the reactions to be thought-forms, but they are mistaken. There is a vast difference, and you will learn to recognize it. A thought-form is a clump of energy, as you will recall, which tends to stay put for a length of time in proportion to the amount of energy put into it. A wave-form, on the other hand, is a transitory phenomenon which spreads throughout the etheric body like the ripples which form in a pond after you toss in a rock. Hence the name. Wave-forms, therefore, unlike the more powerful thought-form, are never capable of assuming a life of their own and almost never affect another person directly. In short, a stranger is not likely to feel pain when you stub your toe.

When we use a radionic device to isolate and work with a wave-form, it is something akin to reaching into the pool of water and pulling out one wave, while leaving all the others intact. The radionic device makes us capable of so specifically tuning our psychic abilities that we are able to seek out and either analyze

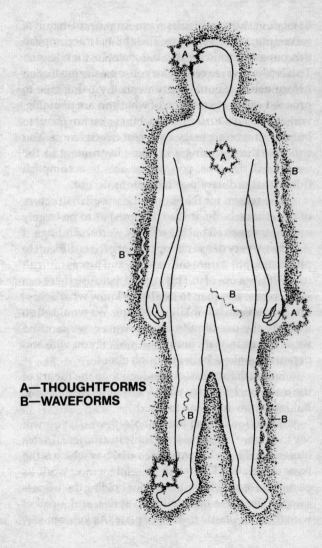

A—THOUGHTFORMS
B—WAVEFORMS

or work with the particular wave-form or collection of wave-forms that we desire. The ability to accomplish this, however, lies in the skill and control of the operator. That is why it was necessary for you to master meditation before using radionic instruments. By being able to proceed with a clear vision of what you are planning, you will be able to use the machines you are about to build both with accuracy and great effectiveness. You will find that by using a radionic instrument in the ways I will describe, you will be able to accomplish things that ordinary psychic actions do not.

The reason for that lies in the peculiar structure of the etheric body. It is so designed as to be largely impenetrable to all but the most powerful sendings. It is, in fact, a very dense clump of energy. It is difficult to put things into it from the outside, and just as difficult to pull things out of it. This is good, because there can be no worse fate than to be able to know what everyone around you is thinking or feeling. We would all go mad. By the use of radionics, however, we can find weak points in that clump, that wall, if you will, and penetrate it like a bullet through cheese.

So much for a basic introduction to the theory of the machine. I will give you a bit more as we go along, but right now it is time to build.

If you look at the illustration (*figure 3*), you will see the layout of the basic radionic instrument. In this illustration I have drawn a three-dial box which is the basic design that I have found useful for most work. Its elements are as follows: the can for holding the witness sample, the three dials wired in series, and a coil of wire under a plastic or rubber plate. As you can see,

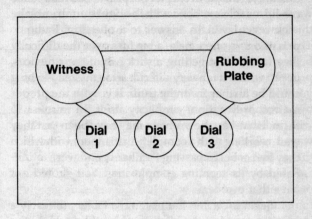

Figure 3

this is an extremely easy machine to build, and at this point you would do well to put one together for yourself and thus be able to experiment with it as I go along. By doing so, you will find that everything will be easier to understand.

Before you begin to build your apparatus, it would be wise to determine if you are going to be able to make it work. This is relatively easy to find out, because the entire practice of radionics depends on the ability to get a "stick" out of the rubbing plate. Therefore, before putting your box together you should acquire the plastic pad you will use for the plate and test yourself.

The rubbing plate, or stick pad as it is sometimes

called, is, in this device, a piece of plastic, such as a coffee can lid, which is rubbed with the right thumb until the stick is achieved, in answer to a question. Radionic practitioners often make a big fuss over the difficulty they had in first getting a stick out of their devices, implying that it is a very difficult art to master. Nothing could be further from the truth. It is, with the proper mental preparation, simplicity itself. In fairness to them, however, the problem may have been that they were working with a complete instrument with which they had at best a passing familiarity and were intimidated by its seeming complexities. You should not have that problem.

Begin by laying the plate on a table, preferably a wooden one, but the kitchen table will do. Hold the plate with your left hand, as in figure 4. Notice that the plate is held firm by the thumb and fore-finger pressing on the edge of the plate. It is wise to avoid placing them directly on top of the plate, not so much because of any interference they will cause in the energy flow which causes the stick, but simply because this position keeps them out of the way.

Now, sit for a minute and take a few deep breaths. Ask yourself a simple question to which you know the answer to be yes. As you do this, gently rub your right thumb across the plate. You should achieve the stick almost immediately. It is difficult to describe just what it feels like, but in my experience it is as if the plate just grabs my thumb and keeps it from sliding. Others report that it feels like they are rubbing over glue. In any event, you will not be able to ignore the feeling when it comes. Sometimes, there is a popping noise associated with it,

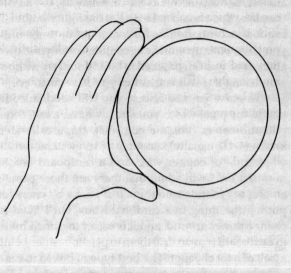

Figure 4

but not always, so do not be disappointed if this does not occur. Likewise, do not be disappointed if nothing happens on the first try. Everyone has a different experience at first, and probably all you need is practice.

Assuming that you have achieved the stick, your next step will be to refine your questioning skills. Take several pieces of paper and write on them four possible answers to a question which has been bothering you. Turn them over and shuffle them so that you do not know what answer is on which paper. Now spread them in front of you and number them one through four. Ask yourself for each one if that is the correct answer, or best answer as the case may be, as you rub the plate. You should get a stick at the right number. It is good to continue this for a number of times until you have built up sufficient confidence in your own abilities so you can proceed to build your box without wondering if it will work after you have finished.

To make your basic box, you will need, in addition to the plate which you already have, a can, three potentiometers (volume controls), three calibrated knobs (1-10, usually), a couple of screws and nuts, a whole pile of copper wire, and a cardboard box to mount it on. I will admit that there are those purists among my friends who think that I am a bit crazy for putting the thing in a cardboard box, but I liked to change things around, and it is easier to punch holes in cardboard than to drill them in plastic besides being a hell of a lot cheaper. The best type of box to use is a gift-type box, usually measuring approximately 12″ x 12″ x 1″. But any box will do. My first machine was put in an old shoe box and it still is in use after some years.

Begin by making your stick plate. Take the plastic plate you have been practicing with and a coil of unshielded copper wire. Coil the wire under the plate so that when turned over, it looks something like figure 5, with the ends of the wire sticking out from one side. It is not necessary to use too much wire for this, a couple of loops will do. Now, simply take a strip of plastic electric tape and stick the wire into place. Put this arrangement to one side.

The sample can is even easier to make. Punch two holes in the bottom of the can and put a screw

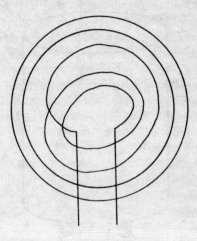

Figure 5

through each, fastening with a nut on the outside. Put this next to the stick plate so you will not have to go searching for it when you need it. It should look like the example in figure 6.

Now comes the fun part. Wire the three potentiometers together in series so that they will look like the three dials in figure 3. It is not necessary to solder the wire to the controls. It is sufficient to wrap the wire tightly around the contacts sticking out from the potentiometers. I know this does not make much sense electrically, but we are not making an electrical device in the true meaning of the word. Put the controls and wire to one side, being careful not to tangle the

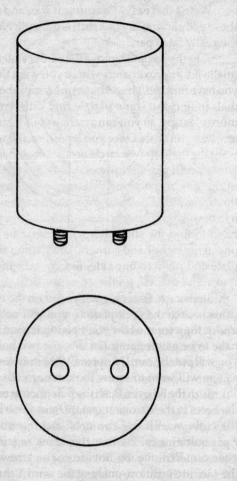

Figure 6

wires connecting them.

Wasn't that easy? Of course it was, and shame on those people who say this stuff is difficult. Now comes the really hard part.

Take the box and remove the lid. Set your three dials on the lid, approximately where you want them when you have finished. I have drawn the sample box with the dials in line, but some people find different patterns more pleasing, so you can arrange your instrument in any way you wish. Once you have decided where you want the dials, draw a circle around each dial onto the lid with your pencil. Now put the knobs into the bottom of the box so they don't disappear when you need them. Place the stick plate onto the lid where you find it to be most convenient. Assuming you use your right hand to find the stick, the plate should be placed in one of the right-hand corners. Draw a line around the plate and put it to one side. Finally, take the can and repeat the process on the opposite side.

Taking your punch, push a hole through the center of each circle where the dials will be. Put two holes under the center of the stick plate location. You may have to be a little careful in this, the two holes where you will put the can. Do not make those holes too large as you will want to screw the can onto the box lid.

Turn the lid over. Push the potentiometers through the holes in their locations, so that the screw is through the other side. Using the small nut that comes with each, bolt it into place. Turn the lid over again and take your can. Remove the nuts from the screws and put the can into position, pushing the screws through the lid and place each nut loosely on the screw inside the lid. Now put the wires from the stick pad through their holes and glue the stick pad into position. Use cellophane tape to hold the pad in place until it hardens.

Take a length of wire and attach it to the screw on the can nearest the stick pad. Tighten that nut securely. Now, repeat the process with the other screw. Take the wire from the stick pad nearest the can and the corresponding can wire and twist them together. Repeat the process with the other wire from the can and the nearest and potentiometer wire. All that remains is to twist the loose stick pad wire with the loose potentiometer wire and your wiring is complete. Now you can put the lid onto the bottom of the box.

All that now remains to complete the instrument is attaching the knobs and setting the calibration. That is also a simple process. Before you put the knobs onto the potentiometer stems, take a ruler and pencil and draw a straight line from the center of the stem out through the top of the circle where the knob is going to be placed. Do this with each potentiometer stem.

Look at the knobs. They will have a small screw which will hold them in place on the stem set into the side. With a small screwdriver or penknife, loosen these screws but do not take them out. They are a royal pain to put back in. Before you put these on, turn each stem as far to the left as it will go without forcing. Now put the first knob onto the stem of a potentiometer. Adjust the knob so that the 'O' is directly over the line you have just drawn. Now tighten the screw. Repeat this process with the remaining two knobs, and your box is now ready for use.

5

How To Make It Work

Congratulations! You have now made a device that has caused controversy and consternation for the better part of this century. Now all you have to do is learn how to use it.

The most important aspect of this machine is the all important *rate*. I have already explained that the rate is nothing more than the numerical equivalent of an individual or animal (or plant or rock or cloud for that matter) as shown by the position of the dials on a radionic box. This rate may indicate the subject as a whole, or merely one aspect of the subject. This fact will become obvious as I show you how to operate the device.

Having decided who you want to get a rate for, let us say Uncle Harry, the first thing you must do is acquire a witness for him. "What's a witness?" I hear you asking. Good question, and one which is rarely given a good answer. A witness, to make something very complicated (in theory at least) rather short and uncomplicated, is anything which will psychically represent the subject. This can be a photograph, signature, blood specimen, hair clipping, nail clipping,

91

anything. In practical terms, a signature or photograph is the most reasonable to obtain and use. It is not likely that you will be able to get blood samples for any purpose, and it is not even necessary. You may, if you have been practicing your concentration exercises, be able to get results with a simple piece of paper with the subject's name written on it. All that is necessary is that there be a link of some kind between the machine and your subject.

Place the witness in the can provided. It is a good idea to keep the can clean. This means dusting it occasionally and never using it to hold crackers when the machine is not in use. Dirt or crumbs have a way of interfering with accuracy of the results you will obtain.

Having done this, sit and meditate for a few minutes. Remember, you are going to be doing somewhat more than merely turning dials, so behave accordingly. It may even help to play a little mad scientist music before you start, just to get you into the right mood. It is also a good idea to keep your activities in this area a secret, as your materialistic friends may not quite understand what you are doing and might try to discourage you. So keep this under your hat, so to speak.

Having prepared yourself for the task at hand, concentrate on the subject. You should be able to keep your thoughts on the subject and what you are trying to determine about him. If you are able to visualize Uncle Harry while working the machine, so much the better, but that is not necessary at this point. Simply do your best to keep distracting thoughts out while getting the rate. It is not, for example, a good idea to have the television on in the background while using the device. Remember, any extraneous thought will be reflected in the results you get, so keep your mind on your subject.

If you have built your machine as I have instructed you, the witness will be at the left-hand side of the machine and the stick plate at the right. When radionic practitioners get together, this is called setting up for right-hand operation. All they are saying is that you are using your right hand to work the stick plate, while tuning the dials with your left.

Sit facing the machine with it resting on a table at a comfortable height. Put your left hand in position, holding the first dial you wish to set as you would any knob on your radio or television. Place your right thumb on the plate. Note that it does not matter which order you use in setting the dials. The rate will come out the same no matter which. I usually work from left to right, while others may do the opposite.

Begin turning the first dial *very* slowly while rubbing your thumb over the stick pad. If you have practiced the use of the pad as I taught you in the last chapter, you will notice the stick when you get it. Continue to turn the dial until you get the stick, and then stop. Repeat this process with the other two dials and you will have your rate for Uncle Harry.

Now that was easy, wasn't it? For most of us, it will be just like that, with no trouble whatsoever. If, however, you were one of the unfortunates who had some difficulty this first time around, despair not, but persevere.

If you failed to get a stick, it could be due to a

number of factors which have nothing whatever to do with either you or the machine. Let us say that you turned the first knob through its entire cycle and did not get the stick. Turn the dial back and try again. If you fail the second time, there are a number of things you can do to try to find the cause of the malfunction.

Different spots on the stick pad tend to be more sensitive than others. You can find the best spot to rub by the simple method of moving your thumb to different places on the pad while you rub it. The one that offers the best resistance is the place you should rub. Once you have found the ideal place for your thumb, try again.

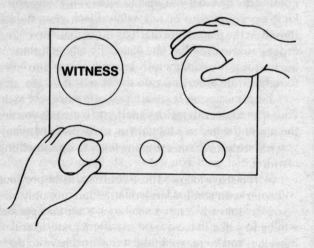

6

Practical Work

Good for you! Due to your diligence and hard work (not too hard, I hope) you now possess the machine which has baffled, confused and annoyed countless researchers for the better part of this century. Let the entrenched neo-Luddites rave to their hearts' content. You now possess the infamous "Box" and there is not a blessed thing they can do about it.

But this creates a question. Now that you have this wondrous device, this wonder of the ages, this *Grand Invention Pour Le Epoch*, what are you going to do with it? After all, if it looks anything like mine, you are not going to try to pass it off as some piece of avant-garde sculpture. You are going to try to do something with it.

If you have followed the instructions in the previous chapter with some degree of attention, not only will you have already learned how to get a rate for a person, but you will also have learned that that rate, in and of itself, is totally meaningless. What you have to do is learn how to narrow that infinite range of possible meanings down to one specific aspect of your subject.

I realize that this sounds terrifying in the abstract.

95

How is this to be done? Well, like most things, when you take them out of the abstract and into the real world, it is a surprisingly uncomplicated matter. Let's use Uncle Harry again.

You begin by making a decision. No one sits down at a radionic device the way they would with the more traditional psychic apparatus, such as a Ouija Board, and just wait for inspiration, or for the answer to mysteriously form itself. Radionics is an active form of psychic activity, and a rather passive one. In that regard, those who have claimed that radionics is in some way akin to the traditional practice of magic are not that far off, in the sense that the old magicians actively moved to influence their world, as opposed to the oracles and mediums who simply let their world act through them. It is an important distinction. When you prepare to use your device, you must realize that it is you, not the machine, that is in control. The box is, after all, nothing but a series circuit which makes not a bit of sense electronically.

So when you sit in front of your array of dials, you have to have first made up your mind as to what you wish to accomplish with this apparatus. Your subject is Uncle Harry. Now, what do you wish the machine to tell you about him?

Suppose your uncle has a habit of twitching his left foot. You wish to find the rate for that habit, or its cause. Decide. You have two very different things here, and your machine can only tell you one. You think for a while and finally come to the conclusion that you want to know the rate for the cause of his habit. Once you have made that decision, and concluded that difficult process, you are ready to get a rate.

Assuming that the witness sample you are using is a picture of Uncle Henry, you will place that picture in the sample can. At this point there are two methods you can use. In most cases, the wisest thing is to write the desired result on a small piece of paper; in this case it would be "Tell me the rate for the cause of twitch in the left foot," and put that into the can with the picture. Some workers in this field think you should write it on the picture itself, but I have found that often you may wish to use the same photograph for different operations, and in that case you do not want writing all over it.

The other method takes a little more work, involving an extra degree of concentration. When using that method, you hold an image of the twitch and its cause in your mind while turning the dials. Once you have become adept at using the machine, this is going to be the method you will most likely use, because it keeps the laboratory from being clogged with little slips of paper, but for now it might be best to write it down first. That way, your mind will be clear for the working of the machine.

Having done this, work your machine the same way that you did after you first built it. That procedure never changes. You always get a rate for the same way. Once you have done this, take a piece of notebook paper and write on it, "Twitch in left foot" and then the rate. This is the beginning of your *Book of Rates*, which is a very important thing to have and which I will return to later.

But first there is a little matter that needs some

clarification. The box you are working with has only three dials, each calibrated from one to ten. This fact, of necessity, limits the number of separate rates you can take. You can, by skillful reading, considerably increase that number. For example, the first dial you turn has been so inconsiderate as to stop halfway between three and four. You mark that rate as 3.5. By doing this, you give your box a far wider range than it would otherwise have. It will take a little practice to be able to guess the exact decimal place of the dial, but you should learn the skill with little difficulty, and if you are a place off on either side, you should realize that there is enough tolerance in the system that such a slight error is not catastrophic. Hence your rate for Uncle Harry's twitch may read something like 3.5, 1.8, 7.4.

Now, you must understand that the machine has not told you the name of the cause of the twitch, merely the rate for the cause. But, as you are not writing a medical journal article, you have no need of that information. In fact, if you wish to attempt a cure for the twitch, you only need the rate, not the name of the cause.

But back to the book of rates. Let us suppose that your Aunt Mathilda has the same twitch, and seeing them sitting together, twitching in unison, is most annoying. So you are naturally curious as to whether or not that twitch may have the same cause. You already have the rate for Uncle Harry's twitch. Place a picture of Aunt Mathilda in the sample can and set the dials for the same rate. Now rub your thumb over the plate. Remember, you can only get two responses.

Either your thumb sticks, or it does not. If it does, then you know, beyond any cause for doubt, that their mutual habit is the result of the same cause. If it does not, which is likely to be the case, the source is different.

At this point you have another decision to make. Do you want to find the rate for Aunt Mathilda's twitch, or are you going to just forget the whole thing and put it down to some congenital nuttiness in that particular branch of the family? If you wish to continue, it is a simple matter, now that you have done it a couple of times, to get the rate for her twitch as well.

After you have done this you have another option. You can, if you wish, stop one or both of them from twitching. Let us say that you have become thoroughly disgusted with your uncle and you wish to stop his annoying habit once and for all without going to the trouble and mess of shooting him. Your machine gives you the option of a less drastic procedure.

Go to your list of rates. I know it is not much of a list right now, but it will grow as you go along. Find the rate for Uncle Harry's twitch. Now here comes the part that is easy to do but nearly impossible to explain why. To find the rate which will cure your uncle, *subtract each of the three numbers from ten*. Thus, if the rate for the twitch is 3.5, 1.8, and 7.4, the curative rate will be 6.5, 8.2 and 2.6. Place Uncle Harry's picture in the can and set the dials to that rate. Now all you need is patience. Given enough time, your uncle will cease his twitching and everyone will be happy.

You are undoubtedly wondering why that should be the case. After all, it does not make any sense to think that a photograph put in a tin can attached to three dials set on a cardboard box is going to cause any result in the subject. I can only say with all honesty that it does, and nobody really knows why. There are many explanations, some of them rather bizarre, as to why any result would be obtained in the first place. There is no reason why I should not try to inflict my own view on the subject on you, so I'll let you decide for yourself if it is worth anything.

I have previously stated that the human body is surrounded by an energy field which goes by any number of names depending on whom you happen to be reading at the moment. There is a relationship between this field and everything which goes on in the body, be it chemical activity in the cells to electrical activity in the brain. This field can be said to bear the same relation to the physical person as the girders to a skyscraper. The field exists first, and the body is hung on it. If that is the case, then any change in this field will result in a similar change in the person. Now, even if that is granted, how is it that a photograph, or even the person's name, can be used to influence that field? I'm afraid that for this explanation, modern science, as good as it is, will not help us very much and will probably only serve to make a muddy issue even less clear by adding terms that nobody can understand, with the exception of specialists who only talk to each other and thus have no idea of how to communicate with the rest of humanity.

The tradition of the magical link is what we are dealing with here, and if we are accused of playing with electronic (sic) voodoo dolls, it is very possible that we deserve to be. In all such traditional magic, the belief that a person's name *is* that person, or that any part of a person is that person (even his picture for that matter), is essential. Certainly we must assume that such a link exists, or it would be obvious that the equipment would not work. As to *how* the link functions, in fact we can only guess. The old ideas that by possessing such a link gives you in some way possession of part of the person is as good a way of looking at as any, and frees you of the necessity of learning the gobbledygook of paraphysical jargon.

I have already explained that it's possible to take a small section of the field and examine it. That is what you did when you found the rate for Uncle Harry's twitch. But there is, we all must admit, a vast difference between examining that portion of the field, which is, after all, no great deal, and directly influencing that same portion of the energy body. Rather than be abstract about it and even confuse myself, I will try to be practical and explain by steps.

When we acquire the link (in this case the photograph), we acquire a *functional* representation of the energy field of that person. This puts us in touch with the person at the level of *his* energy body because it permits our own energy fields to make the necessary connection. If I may use an overworked and rather bad analogy, it is like putting a tuning crystal into a radio receiver. Now, there are receivers which do not use crystals to tune them, and you will have guessed by now that the link is not always necessary, but having one makes things a lot easier. In any event, having the link makes it possible to work with the energy body of the subject. This is always the case.

Once the link has been made, you are able, at the level of your own subconscious, to contact that person or any aspect of that person. You are, in effect, wired to that person in the same way your telephone is wired to other telephones. All that is necessary is to punch the number. At this point, your box comes in because it reduces the abstract thought-form with which you may be dealing, or the even more abstract wave-form, to a series of numbers on a dial, in exactly the same way that the mathematical relationship between voltage and current is shown by the dial on an electric meter. Now this creates a different relationship between the operator, you, and the subject, Uncle Harry. Where before you may have been close to your Uncle and may even have occasionally had some telepathic instances regarding him in the same way my Great Aunt Lula knew when disaster struck her distant relation, now, by means of the box, you have not only the normal contact you would have had without it, but also a narrowing of the range of that contact. Instead of getting a series of impressions willy-nilly, like a radio psychic, you are able to deal with one highly specific aspect of your uncle: his twitch.

But none of this, while it explains how you are able to get a rate, tells you *why* the box is able to transmit back to Uncle Harry and why his twitch should be cured by that transmission. The answer to this lies in the link and the specificity of the rate.

Remember, in the traditional view, the link is the person. If the witch doctor sticks pins into a doll with the link as a part of it, he is, for all practical purposes, sticking pins into the subject. The reason most people are unable to get any results from repeating that operation is they have not had the mental training to be able then to make the link with subject more specific. The box works in the same way, but hopefully to different ends. The picture of Uncle Harry is always the link, no matter if the box is receiving or transmitting. As long as his picture is in the can, he is locked into whatever is coming out of the box, just as if his phone were lying off the hook while somebody else was talking to him. As long as the phone is off the hook and the line is open, the voice is going to come out the other end.

By taking a rate, the rate itself becomes a representational link with that portion of the energy body, so now you have a link not only with Uncle Henry but also with that portion of his field which is causing the twitch. In fact, if you were to leave this rate on the machine with your uncle's picture, the amplifying effect of the box would make his twitch worse. But when you put the cure rate onto the box, you are now linked to Uncle Harry and sending to him a corrective, or as some operators say, balancing rate, which will automatically work on his energy body and bring the twitch under control and ultimately eliminate it. This occurs because the corrective rate is specifically the opposite of the twitch rate.

The whole thing is linked to the peculiar nature of the circuitry of the box, and how that circuitry works. As you can see from figure 7, the circuit runs from the witness of Uncle Harry, through the box where the signals is refined, to you by way of the stick

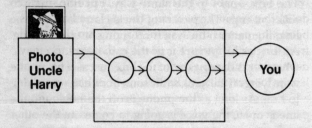

Figure 7

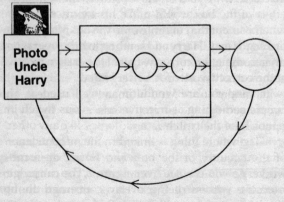

Figure 8

pad. But once you are removed from the system, the circuit takes the refined signal from the box back to Uncle Harry as illustrated in figure 8.

Now I can just hear you thinking (which by the way is a good habit to get into and more people should do it) that if you, by working the stick pad and thus becoming part of the system, can pick up the signal from Uncle Harry, isn't it possible that you too may develop the infamous twitch? The answer is no, or at least, not very likely. Radionics, if it has one disadvantage, is that it does require a certain amount of exposure. The length of time you spend with your thumb stroking the plate is so short that it is insufficient for thought of the particular energy you are working with to leak through to you. You are perfectly safe. It is something similar to taking a photograph but not letting the film get enough exposure.

After you have set the box for the corrective rate, put it aside for a while—at least until you see Uncle Harry again. You should, at that time, notice that *his* twitch has departed and now only Aunt Mathilda is twitching. It may be a good idea to repeat the operation with her, using the corrective rate for her own twitch, not the corrective rate for Uncle Harry.

In case you are wondering why I used as an example something as minor as a nervous twitch in the foot, I should explain that radionics, like any other psychic activity, requires a certain amount of confidence in the outcome. By deliberately working on something very obvious but not very serious, you can judge the results without being overly concerned about them. It is best to start with simple things and work out any bugs which you may encounter before trying something really big, like the Slobovian Flu.

Another thing you will notice is that I do not instruct you to tell the subject you are performing your little experiment. There are two very good reasons for this. First, you want to be certain the results are there because of the machine, not because of the subject healing himself by what is now termed the "Placebo Effect." Secondly, a person can get into a lot of trouble for making people well without a license. In fact this is a good time to give you a word of warning. *NEVER,* UNDER ANY CIRCUMSTANCES, TAKE MONEY FROM *ANYONE* FOR USING THE MACHINE IN ANY WAY. In fact, it is a good idea to never let anyone know that you are using the machine for them.

Now I realize that I am flying in the face of the principles followed by most radionic practitioners. In fact, in England, the Radionic Association is most strict in its belief that no one should be treated without his or her consent. My answer to that is quite simple. This is not England, and the ethical principles of the Radionic Association are based on a naivete which is charming in children but rather silly in the real world. I may have a few more comments about them later.

It is not only living things that can be analyzed by the radionic device, but also minerals as well, though in these cases you need not be concerned about the transmitting role of the device. Let us say that you have a ring and you would like to know if it contains real gold. This is easily done. Merely take some piece of jewelry that you definitely know has gold and put it in the can. Identify the rate and write it into your book.

That is very important. Never forget to write down each rate you take. It can save you some trouble later on. Remove the test piece from the can, also very important; and, leaving the box at the gold rate, test again with the stick pad. If there is gold in the ring, you will get a stick. If not, you may have been cheated, so you should take the ring to a jeweler and have it checked again.

The same procedure can be used to find minerals in water or soil and even test the purity of food, though the last should only be done on an experimental basis with the option of having the sample tested by more conventional means. There are times when you do not want to risk being wrong, though with experience the number of your mistakes will decrease.

But let us get back to people. Not only is the box useful for dealing with physical conditions or behavior, but it is even more useful when dealing with thoughts and emotions. Yes, Bunky, you too can read minds.

The procedure is similar to that of finding a rate for a physical condition. Let us say you wish to determine if person X really loves person Y. You first have to get a rate for love. Now love, as we all know, can take many forms, so you should be certain to use for a witness someone emanating the type of love you wish to isolate. Failing that, it is possible for you to use the word 'love' written on a piece of paper for your witness.

Put this witness in the can and get a rate for it. Remove the witness, but leave the setting on the dials. Remember to write this rate down in your book. After doing that, take a piece of paper and write the names of person X and person Y on it and place this in the can. Now try the stick plate. If the relationship between them fulfills the idea placed in the system by the witness, you should get a stick. If you do not, it can mean a number of things.

First, you may have used the wrong witness. Your example of love may not have been at all what you really had in mind and thus you took a correct rate for that particular witness, but that was not the one you were really looking for.

Second, the relationship that exists between your subjects may very well be love in any number of the uses of the word, but not the type you are asking about. Again, you have the right answer to the wrong question. It is very important to be as specific as possible when using the machine in this manner.

Third, they really do not love each other in any sense of the word and you have been indulging in the sort of games popular with pre-adolescent girls and should be ashamed of yourself. (Just kidding)

It *is* possible to be even more detailed in your study of this interesting couple. Suppose you wish to find out if the feeling is shared by both parties, or only present in one.

Write the name of each party on a separate slip of paper. Place the slip bearing the name of X into the can and try the stick pad. If it sticks, then he is fulfilling the conditions of your question. If there is no stick, he is not. Repeat the procedure with Y.

As you can imagine, this procedure can be of great use to you in your personal life. In my own case, I was deeply involved with a young woman who, in spite of her many protestations of affection, did not, in fact, seem to be as carried away with me as her words implied. I naturally found this state of affairs to be both confusing and highly troublesome. I couldn't take her at her word, and yet to continue the relationship seemed a fruitless task, for it had become just that, a task. Using the machine, I was able to determine that she was not so much lying to me as to herself, and it was thus only a matter of time before she came to her senses and realized that the situation could not continue. I, for my part, was now relieved of a great concern and was able to continue my life without being unduly bothered by the inconsistent behavior of this person. The matter came to its obvious conclusion and I was, by being forewarned, spared the usual traumas that come with such occurrences.

The machine, due to its yes/no function can also serve as an excellent lie detector. The procedure is surprisingly simple and I am amazed that, to my knowledge, it has not been published before. It must be understood that when a person tells a deliberate lie, his body will react by sending off a number of signals. This is why a polygraph can work, though because of its nature it can also give inaccurate readings which can cause a lot of trouble for the persons involved. A radionic device picks up more than the mere physical readings of the polygraph. It picks up changes in the energy body and these are much more reliable as indicators of truth than sweaty palms and increased respiration.

To begin this operation, it is first necessary to get a rate for "truth." This is easier than it may seem at first thought. All you have to do is write the word "truth" on a slip of paper and drop it into the can. You then take your rate and record it. I should disgress and mention at this point that some operators assign rates for such things, by simply telling themselves that 001 is the rate for truth, for example, and checking the stick pad. I think that for a beginner it is better to take a rate in the usual manner. By doing so, you are allowing your subconscious to tell you which rate it will best respond to.

After you have this rate, it is a simple matter to use the machine. Let us say that a certain politician notorious for his duplicity is going to make a speech on television that evening. Write his name on a slip and put it in the machine. Then, while watching him on television, test the pad each time he says something you wish to question. If he is telling the truth as he sees it, you will get a stick. If he's lying, you will not. You must remember, however, that this procedure is telling you what is going on in the mind of the subject. The statement may turn out to be totally false, but if the subject *believes* it to be true, the machine will tell you he is not lying. The fault, in that case, is neither in the subject nor the machine, but in the information the subject has.

I have found this method to be useful in dealing with matters of more pressing concern than the election of a new sewer commissioner. In dealing with individuals on the telephone, I have found it useful to have my machine set up on the desk in front of me. When doing this, I make a practice of getting the name of the person on the other end and writing it quickly and inserting it into the can.

By now you should have a pretty good idea of the basic method, so before we leave the box for a little bit, I will only give you one more basic use. It will be of some importance to you as you progress, so pay attention.

Up to now, we have been primarily concerned with finding the rate of a certain aspect of a given person, be it in his physical or emotional make-up. There is, however, a more general rate that applies to each individual, and that is his personal rate. Now, the personal rate is nothing more than the rate at which the machine is best attuned to the individual as a whole, and is of great use in telepathy experiments. It is sometimes called the contact rate because of this feature.

In the period immediately following the end of the Second World War, there were so many predictions about what the world would be like in the near future that it quickly became fashionable to satirize them. One of these satires took the form of an editorial cartoon by Ding Darling, a famous cartoonist of the period in which a scientific-looking gentleman is showing a rather dumpy-looking woman a complicated box with binoculars affixed to its top and telling her that with this machine she will be able to tune in on her husband's personal wavelength and know what he was up to at all times. Mr. Darling thought he was being funny, but it turns out that the joke was on him. Not only does everyone *have* what can be called a personal wavelength, but even as he was drawing that cartoon, someone was working on a device which would accomplish exactly that. Unfortunately, the devices produced by the de la Warr laboratories in Great Britain are way outside the purview of this book and so we will have to leave the discussion of the de la Warr camera to those more competent to speak of it. We are going to be more concerned with the somewhat mundane practices of telepathy and remote viewing.

By now you are probably getting furious with me and demanding that I get to the point. Okay. The personal rate is very simple. As I have just said, it is the rate at which your mind, as the operator of your machine, is most clearly in touch with that part of your subject which is most receptive to being contacted, something like finding the clearest point of tuning for a FM stereo receiver. Once you have this rate for a given individual, you can send him a telepathic message with much greater clarity than you would by the usual means of transmission. Your way of working will be much the same, but you will be tuned in to your target with more precision.

Let us try a little experiment to illustrate what I am getting at. For this experiment, you will need a person who has a big mouth, one who will talk to you, or anyone else for that matter, about anything, including what he or she dreamt the night before.

Taking the personal rate is very simple. Assume that your subject is your long-suffering aunt Mathilda, who is coming over tomorrow for dinner with Uncle Harry, he of the former twitch. Take the witness of your aunt and put it in the can with a small piece of paper on which you have written the words "personal rate." The paper, incidentally, does not serve any other purpose than to aid you in concentrating on the reason for the operation. It need not be saved after you have the rate. Once you have taken and recorded the rate, take out your pendulum (you remember, from a couple of chapters ago). Set the box so that you can sit with one hand on the plate and the other, holding the pendulum, near the wall, so that it will strike the wall if swung. Ideally the left hand should be on the plate and the pendulum in your right. Have you got that? Good. Now ask the pendulum to tell you what time Aunt Mathilda will be asleep—not when she is going to bed, but when she will be asleep. Let's assume the pendulum strikes once. If that's the case, you can go out and play because you have nothing to do until 1 a.m. At the appointed hour, take out the pendulum again and ask it if Aunt Mathilda is asleep. If it says yes, then you can proceed with the experiment.

With your hand on the box, close your eyes and begin to meditate, just as you have learned. While you do this, see your aunt in your mind. You are now creating a very strong telepathic link between yourself and your aunt. Later on, I will discuss instruments which will make this link even stronger, but for our purposes right now, you are in insufficient contact to influence her dreams.

This can be tricky. I should warn you in advance that the subconscious mind, which is what we are working with here, can take its own turns and surprise even those of us who have been at this for years. A good thing to work on is some strong feeling, such as hunger. Remember, you are going to want her to talk about her night, so you have to make it something she will talk about. While holding your aunt in concentration, begin to think about food, any food. You want to think about this so strongly that after a few minutes you will have to get up and get a snack for yourself. When that occurs, the experiment is ended and you should put the equipment away and not worry about it until your aunt arrives the next day. Then, during the usual chit-chat, bring up the subject of late-night eating.

Using the box as an aid in the practice of remote viewing is a bit more difficult. It takes a little practice and time, so be patient. In case you do not know what the term "remote viewing" means, it is the ability to mentally see things which are distant with enough accuracy that you can cause those who were actually there to become very surprised. It is the talent that the researchers at the turn of this century called "traveling clairvoyance," so if you should run into that phrase in an old book, you know what they were talking about.

There are a number of experiments now being conducted with this faculty, some of them yielding very interesting results, and some of them best forgotten. Unfortunately, for the purposes of most people, the method of experiment is such that the average person would be discouraged from developing the faculty rather than pursuing it. After all, who wants to pick out a location on a map and try to see what's there. But remote viewing has an extremely practical aspect, and I would encourage anyone to take the time and trouble to learn how to use it.

Before I explain how to use the box in this regard, I have to teach you how to perform the basic activity. While it may take some time to get your best results, the practice itself is rather simple.

You already know how to meditate, and I hope you have been practicing it with some regularity. And that is how we begin. You will use the methods of meditation to focus your mind on the target; in this case let's say it is your mother. When you do this you will get a visual image in your head of your mother. Now this image can be of something you remember, such as seeing her watching television, or something different, something she is doing at the moment you are concentrating on her. The latter is what you are after, so close your eyes, and try to see her in your mind; try to hold her image while willing yourself to see what she's doing now. Once you get an image, try to hold on to it. Look around, try to get as much detail as possible. If she is at home, concentrate on what she is doing.

For this experiment, as in most others, it is best to use someone you are quite close to. It makes verification much easier. After you come back, as it were, it is a simple matter to give your mother a call and ask her. That method is much easier than drawing a picture, especially if your drawing skills are anything like mine.

That was simple, wasn't it? I remember my first experience with the technique. A friend of mine and I were waiting for a third person, and she was a bit late. Being naturally curious as to the reason for this, my friend suggested that we try a bit of psychic research. We both closed our eyes and looked for her. And wonder of wonders! We found her, in her car, driving the wrong way! After that, we did not expect her, and it later turned out that she had an emergency errand to run and was in her car going to that place while we were looking in on her. You must admit that this type of experiment is much more practical than trying to describe a unique feature of the landscape around James Bay.

You should practice this method, without the machine, several times. That way you will get the basics down before going on.

When you feel that you are finally getting the hang of remote viewing, it is time to use the machine. Choose the subject you wish to view and obtain a witness sample. By now people should be used to you running around with a camera taking everyone's picture, so you can get one easily enough. Having done this, put the picture into the can and get a contact rate. Place your left hand on the plate of the machine and close your eyes. Begin to meditate, visualizing the person in the can. If things are going right, you will get an immediate impression which should be much clearer than you have obtained in the past. In fact, the results may be so clear as to be a bit scary. At this juncture, it no longer is a good idea to ask people directly what they were doing when you saw them doing it. Not everyone is as dedicated to psychic research as we are, and there are those who might get a little upset at the thought of their privacy being violated. Fortunately, most people like to talk, and it is a simple matter to direct a conversation in such a manner that they will tell you everything you need to know without their even knowing they've done it.

Practice with people for a while. I have found from my own experiences that they are the most interesting of subjects. Only after you have worked with them will you be ready for the next step, which is looking at locations and watching what is going on there.

The most difficult part of location, or area, work with radionics is obtaining a good witness sample. A photograph is by far the best and if you have them, old vacation slides, or even movie frames, are excellent for this type of operation. Failing that, photographs cut from old newspapers or magazines will work. By far the best, if you can get your hands on them, are aerial photographs. Place the picture in the can and take a rate. For this purpose, the best procedure is to write the words "Remote Viewing" on a slip of paper and put it into the can with the picture. After you have the rate, you will proceed much in the same manner as you did with your human targets. For verification, try to look around and see things which might be considered newsworthy. This can be a bit difficult, but if you should see something on that order, you can then go to the public library and find a newspaper from that region, assuming you are near a large enough library, and find a story about it; or, failing that, look for some distinctive structure or rock or anything likely to be a travel book but which is not in your witness sample. There will be something. It is simply a matter of finding it.

Once you have become adept at remote viewing, you will have little trouble finding uses for the talent, so I need not detail them. And now we are going to leave the box for a little while, while we look at some other devices and techniques before we come back to the machine.

7

To Stay Healthy

The subject of psychic healing is one which always produces some trouble in the mind of a writer. There is always the fear that a zealous reader will take the advice given to him and then do something stupid, like give up insulin for his diabetes. Therefore, in putting this information before you, I am going to expect that you will use some common sense in its application.

Let me illustrate what I expect you to avoid. At one time in my life I found myself hanging around with a group of religious-type people, and a faith healer came to town. Being of a somewhat skeptical bent, I was unimpressed by his habit of pouring oil on people and pronouncing them cured of everything from arthritis to the dreaded spotted nose-drip. As you may well expect, my lack of faith was a great trial to my friends (and those who still remember me may go into fits over this book) but they came to appreciate my point of view after one of their number who had been copiously greased with olive oil announced that his eyes were healed, threw away his glasses and drove into a tree on his way home.

I insist that you not make the same mistake. If you

are under medical care for anything, do not, even if your pendulum, stick pad, instincts and the sacred chickens say you are healed, give up either your medicine or your doctor. The last thing that I want to run into on the astral plane is the spirit of one of my readers who died because he refused to use his brains.

So how do you use the abilities taught in this book to keep your body in good health? The same way you would use conventional medicine; that is to say, by prevention of what *can* be prevented, and treatment of that which is not. It is far easier from the psychic point of view to prevent illness than it is to treat yourself after you have come down with something. The reason for this should be obvious. All psychic activity requires the ability to concentrate, and concentration is impossible when you are coughing. Believe me, I know. So we will begin with prevention.

You start by resolutely avoiding paranoia. Now by this I do not mean that you are in any great danger of becoming a hypochondriac in the normal sense of the term, but you must face the fact that we live in a hypochondriacal society. If you make a habit of watching television, particularly the network variety, you are being constantly besieged by messages of illness, potential illness and possible cures—usually in the form of some over-the-counter medicaments. In addition, many local stations have their own version of Doctor Guiltgiver, who reports on all the latest plagues, their symptoms and what the viewer can do to avoid them (usually by avoiding something the viewer enjoys doing). As H. L. Mencken said, "In the heart of every Puritan lies the fear that someone somewhere might be happy."

As if this were not bad enough, there is the disease of the weekly TV movie and the ubiquitous commercials which, if viewed with a discerning eye, would give one the unfailing impression that the nation's senior citizens have teeth that do not fit, are always constipated and not potty trained. It would be funny, and often is, but for the fact that even granting you are smart enough not to believe anything that is said on television, the continuous bombardment of this garbage is eating away at your subconscious, which is exactly what the perpetrators of this felony want to happen. They are hoping that if you are not sick when the program comes on, you will be by the time it is over.

I do not expect you to become an anti-television fanatic; in fact, I hope you avoid becoming one, but I want you to be aware of the effects of watching too many commercials. As you are likely to end up seeing your share of these little doses of brainwashing anyway, the most important thing that you can do is learn to neutralize their power.

In order to do this, you will have to practice a bit of auto-suggestion, training your sub-conscious mind to reject the commercial as soon as it makes its noisome presence felt. It is a very simple procedure, and if you have been practicing the lessons thus far you should have no trouble.

Begin with a simple meditation. Repeat your mantra, and continue to do so until you have achieved a totally relaxed state. Once you have done this, begin to repeat a command to yourself, something on the order of "Television is a pack of lies and I believe nothing that is said on it," or "Medicine commercials are for the sick, but I am well and do not hear them." You get the idea. You want to armor your mind so that the message will bounce off you without leaving any mark. It is very important that you do this, because by removing the mental threat, you will make avoiding the physical threats that much easier.

Having dealt with that unfortunate problem, let us now turn to the more pleasant subject of protecting your self from the onset of disease. There are three basic methods of performing this operation: 1) strengthening the etheric body, 2) creating a protective thought-form and 3) radionics.

The process of strengthening your etheric body to resist disease is accomplished through visualization. You should be quite practiced in most of these techniques by now, so this procedure should give you no trouble at all.

As you learned in the last chapter, a disease will appear in the etheric body before it manifests in the physical one. The length of time prior to its physical appearance will vary, with hereditary malfunctions being present for a long time, while a virus may only show up as a weakness in the etheric body which will allow the bug to attack as soon as it gets into the physical system. Every etheric body has its weaknesses, otherwise we would never get sick, and I should warn you that it is very difficult to eliminate them all. You must not feel as if you have sometimes failed just because you find yourself in bed for a few days. You must never fall prey to the malady which affects those who place such faith in the power of *their* particular healing method that they condemn themselves if something doesn't go exactly as planned. By now you have probably discovered that in the area of psychic activity many things don't go exactly as planned. Fear not, it will work more often than it fails, and you will end up by enjoying far better health than your neighbors.

So, start to visualize. You will want to see yourself surrounded by your etheric body, glowing with perfect health. I'd say radiant health, but that can lead to bad jokes about people that live too close to nuclear reactors. Anyway, you understand. Feel the energy of the universe filling your etheric body and making it glow with a brilliant, white light. As you do this, know that all the waveforms that leave you open to disease are being cleaned out; washed away as it were, and you are now invulnerable to the bugs which float around us continually. You should repeat this procedure with some regularity, depending upon your own health and the circumstances. For example, someone who works out of his house would have to only do this once a week, while a person who deals with the public, as in a store, may have to do it as often as twice a day. Certain weather conditions must also be taken into account. A cool, damp day requires more protection than a bitter cold one, because germs like water droplets.

The use of a thought-form to protect your health requires a bit more work and is probably best reserved for those times when a disease of some sort is making the rounds, usually during what is commonly termed the flu season, even though the flu does not follow the calendar. Now I know that there are writers who suggest that you can make a health-protecting thought-form for general use, but my own experience has found that strengthening the etheric body seems to work better for that purpose, though there is certainly no danger in using both. Always be willing to experiment.

By now you should be quite adept at making thought-forms, so you should have little trouble in making this one. Let's assume that in the place where you work, there has been an outbreak of severe stomach colds. You already have your field in place, so you are not particularly concened about catching the dread virus, but you would like to be certain. You would therefore meditate and create a thought-form, giving it the specific instruction that it will block the disease as it attempts to enter your body. Be certain to charge this thought-form daily, to keep it at its maximum power. Assuming that you have done this correctly, you should be able to continue with your life while all around you people are dropping from the bug.

If you thought that using a thought-form is easy, wait until you use your box to protect yourself. Remember that every illness shows up in the etheric body before it manifests in the physical one. This fact can't be repeated too often. Therefore, it follows that if you can keep your etheric body free from the waveforms and thought-forms which weaken it, you should be able to avoid most difficulties, at least in the matter of health. While the strengthening of your etheric body will block individual ailments that appear to be most threatening, the radionic box can seek out and eliminate those weakness which are present and may lead to trouble later on, perhaps years from now.

When doctors first began studying Radionics,

they discovered that there were certain conditions present in practically everyone they diagnosed. They came to the conclusion that these conditions were present in the environment, and while most radionic practitioners agree they are present, they disagree violently about their source, some claiming that they come from the ground, others going so far as to say that they are the result of previous incarnations, though how they would prove this is open to question. Anyway, there is agreement that there are at least three, though again they argue over *which* three. Abrams listed them as Cancer, Tuberculosis and Syphilis. You can imagine the furor the last one caused. Treating infants for Syphilis indeed! To make matters worse, by Syphilis, Abrams was not referring to the venereal disease. Personally, I think too much fuss is made over the "miasms" as these are called. The most important thing is to avoid hypochondria. The surest way to create a disease thought-form is to worry about it. Therefore, when you begin to use the box, your attitude toward any speciic condition you may come up with should be that the condition does *not* exist now and may never show up, but there is no danger in protecting yourself from it. It's something like buying insurance. Just because your policy covers fire doesn't mean that your house is going to burn down.

Protective radionics can be done two ways: the long, complicated way, which is done by experienced practitioners in which the major organs of the body are studied to find weaknesses, and then ultimately the specific weaknesses are dealt with; or the short, easy way, in which the entire etheric body is balanced.

There is a middle way, which is what I am going to teach you.

You will need your pendulum, your box and a photograph of yourself, the more recent the better. You will also need your pendulum chart. It will help if you know a little of your family's medical history as well.

As you probably know, many conditions are hereditary. If your father died of a heart attack, it is a good idea for you to take care of your ticker. The first thing that you will want to do is learn what type of hereditary ailments, if any, have appeared in your family. Once you have done this, make a list of them and place this list on the table in front of you. Place the pendulum chart before you and put your picture either on the center of the chart, or above it.

With the pendulum in your right hand, hold it over the chart as you normally would, and point with your left hand to each condition on your list. If the condition is present in your etheric body, the pendulum will swing positive. At each positive response, mark the condition so you will remember it later. After you have gone through the entire list, you will know what conditions need fixing. Write each of these on a small piece of paper, one condition per piece.

You now have a list of potential conditions which result from heredity. Take each condition and place it above the pendulum chart, one at a time. For each one, ask the pendulum to tell you the strength of the condition in your etheric body, with 0 being no significant potential (unlikely, as you received a positive response from the pendulum before) to 100, being that the condition has just killed you (equally unlikely).

Normally, if you get a pendulum reading under 20, that means that the condition is so weak that there is very little cause for concern. If the reading is over 75, you should get yourself to a physician for a check-up, because the condition may be manifesting in your physical body. Between 20 and 75, you should use the box to treat it. We will come to that soon, but first we must cover the most general method of balancing the etheric body.

In the previous chapter, I explained the technique used for balancing a particular condition (Uncle Harry's twitch) with the radionic box. When the box is used to balance the etheric body, the same procedure is followed, only no specific condition is mentioned. All that you need do is take a rate for yourself, by placing a photograph of yourself in the witness can with nothing else. The rate that you will then obtain is the general rate for your etheric body. By balancing *this* rate, you are then balancing your entire etheric body; at least the general condition of that body at the time the rate was taken. It is wise to repeat this procedure about once a week to adapt to any changes that may have occurred in the meantime. If you are going to use this procedure, it is wise to make a separate machine, because you will want to leave your witness in the system.

But suppose you have found a pre-existent condition that you want to get rid of, or have, in spite of your best efforts, come down with the latest virus? For these, it is best to use the box for the reason that I have already alluded to; namely, concentration can be next to impossible when ill. The treatment procedure is the same as I have outlined in the previous chapter, with one addition. Let us say that you have a sore throat. As with Uncle Harry's twitch, you will write the condition on a small piece of paper, and place that paper in the can with your witness sample. But when you take your rate, try to see your throat while turning the dial. This is easier than it sounds, and with a little practice you should have no trouble accomplishing it. After all, you should know what your own throat looks like. It is not necessary to concentrate on this image, you just want to program yourself to get the rate for your sore throat. Once you have that rate, balance it as you learned to in the last chapter and wait. In a short time, about a day, you should feel better. Sometimes, the box will work almost immediately, but you should not expect this, and don't be disappointed if it takes a little while to work. There are a lot of unknown factors involved in this practice.

Another method which you may use is to write a command on the paper, such as "Heal my sore throat," and place this in with the witness sample. If you use this method, you will simply take a rate and leave that rate on the box. I suggest that you experiment and discover which works best for you. I have used both and find that for me they work equally well.

Once you've set your machine by either method, use your pendulum and chart to find the strength of the condition you are trying to heal. It is a good idea to leave the box set at the curative rate until the pendulum reads 0. I remember one time, when I needed the box for another operation, I took the rate off and the bug came back the next day, so do not just go by your feelings. Another good practice is to reset the machine every couple days until the condition is out of your etheric body. This is done by rebalancing or taking a new curative rate.

Allow me to close this chapter with a few other comments. Psychic healing and radionics are no substitute for normal medicine, and I don't care *what* their more enthusiastic advocates say. If you come down with a serious illness, go to your doctor for treatment and take your medicine. Use the box as well, but follow the doctor's instructions. You can't hurt yourself by using the box as I have instructed you, but unless one is an experienced practitioner in the realm of medical radionics (and there are damned few of them in this country), it is extremely unwise to totally depend on the box for your well-being. Look at it as a useful tool, not as a miracle machine, and always apply a healthy dose of common sense when dealing with your health.

One other thing: it is not a good idea to mention to your doctor that you are using these techniques. Some medical people get very upset at the mere mention of radionics.

8

Gadgets

The radionic box, as you have discovered by now, is a wonderful instrument, and a tremendous number of unusual things can be accomplished by skillful use of it. In and of itself, however, it is not completely sufficient to accomplish everything you will want to do. It is often necessary to supplement your basic box with other devices, and these can be used either alone or in conjunction with the box.

The first of these contraptions has a problem in connection with it. The machine is called the 'teleflasher' and the most serious difficulty involved in using it is that it does not work.

WHAT!

That's right. It does not work, at least in the way it has been touted as *supposed* to work. Oh, it's just fine for playing little psychic games with people who know that you are using the teleflasher and, if the wind is coming out of the right direction, you might even be able to send a one-word message to somebody who does not know that he is on the receiving end of such an experiment. But the teleflasher as it is described in most books on the subject is virtually useless for the purposes of this book.

Now by this time you are probably wondering why I would waste your time, and mine, on something that does not seem to be worth the trouble of making. Well, hold on. I said that it is useless as it is described in most literature on the subject. By the time I am through telling you how to work it, you will discover that the teleflasher is an excellent *supplement* to your box.

Before I tell you how to make one of these machines I am going to explain to you just what the teleflasher is, how it works and why my modification will work better than the conventional versions. Pay attention to this. It may seem a little dry, but learning about this stuff is worthwhile in and of itself and will help you when you set about to design your own devices, as I am certain some of my more adventurous readers are going to do.

I first came across the teleflasher some years ago in a book by Sheila Ostrander and Lynn Schroeder, entitled *Handbook of Psychic Discoveries*. They went into great detail describing this machine, what it does, why they thought it does what it does, or is claimed to do, and telling how to build it. They claim the invention of the device had its roots in research done in the Soviet Union. Now right away, this should cause some grave doubts to form in the mind of any serious researcher. After all, these were the people who claimed to invent everything from fire and the wheel on. If you combine the somewhat inflated claims that come out of Russia with the joyous credulity of some Americans you can get a terrible mess of stories, most incapable of being investigated. This is a very bad situation, because it gives a great deal of ammunition to those who think anything involving the psychic is hogwash.

Anyway, enough disgression. The teleflasher is basically an instrument which uses a flashing light to cause the mind of the person using it to transmit images in quick pulses. And there seems to be no question that this pulsing light will aid in telepathic transmission. Unfortunately, problems can arise when transmitting anything complicated. If you are going to send the number two to somebody sleeping in the next room, you will have little trouble. If you are trying any of the sort of experiments we are talking about, you are going to have some difficulties.

The problems lie in two areas: the conditions of working the device, and the design of the device itself.

To properly use the teleflasher can be quite an interesting task for someone who lacks experience in telepathy experiments. In order to get any kind of appreciable results, you have to be able to first get into a meditative state. After you have done this (and by now you should be able to do this without difficulty), you must be able to concentrate on the image being flashed at you. This is not as easy as it sounds. The creators of the miraculous teleflasher forgot that the pupils of the eyes open and close with light, so when each time the light flashes, they close a little, and the resulting effect can destroy concentration. There is a way to avoid that problem, or at least lessen it and I will tell you about it when we get to my version of the machine.

While you are battling with the flashing light you

have to not only concentrate on the image before you, but also on your target. You have to be able to hold two images in your mind at the same time and that is easier said than done. In addition to that, you must also be able to send, or know that you are sending, the image to the target.

You can easily see what a difficult proposition using the teleflasher can be. Now, add to these problems one very serious design flaw.

The teleflasher is basically nothing but a box with a flashing light inside which illuminates a word or picture. The conventional teleflasher is very good at illuminating words, but is useless with most pictures. Why should this be? A simple teleflasher can be made using a slide sorter, with a flasher plug attached. The message or picture to be sent is placed against the illuminated screen and the light flashed around it, causing the word to stand out in silhouette. This means that anything being sent must be adaptable to this form of lighting. You cannot, for example, transmit a picture from a newspaper. A photograph would be likewise useless. It might be possible to use a slide, but unless you were using a modified slide viewer, it would be hardly practical.

Faced with the above difficulties, it is amazing that anyone is able to get any results at all with the conventional mechanism, and these results are probably useless for anything but testing.

With my method, you eliminate these difficulties. We begin by making a simple modification to the box itself. In figure 9, you will notice that the light box does not stand up, but lies flat, with the light coming up out of the top. You can easily make this by taking an old shoe box and cutting out the bottom. Over the empty hole where the bottom used to be, glue a sheet of translucent plastic. The type used to cover windows in the winter will do nicely. If that isn't available, or is somewhat inconvenient, wax paper will also work. Go to the hardware store and buy a lightbulb socket, with cord and switch attached. While you are there, pick up a 25-watt bulb and a flasher plug. When you get home, cut a hole in the side of the box just big enough for the socket and fit it in. Screw in the bulb, inside the box because it will not work right if the bulb is on the outside. Attach the flasher plug to the cord, plug it in the nearest outlet, and turn on the switch. You will get a dull glow for a few seconds and then the bulb will begin to flash on and off in a more or less regular rhythm.

It has been suggested that you should punch air holes in the sides of the box. I have never found this to be necessary, if only for the simple reason that a flashing light does not get hot enough to cause any problems, and the light escaping from such holes can be very distracting.

Now that you have an idea of how the light will come out the translucent screen, you have to make a stand for the message. Take a piece of thin cardboard, the bottom of the box will do, or a piece of poster board can be used. Bend this so that it will stand at the end of the box as in figure 9. Glue it in place and wait until the glue hardens.

Okay, now that you have a teleflasher, what are you going to do with it? Well, you aren't going to play bingo. Remember the dream experiment in the last

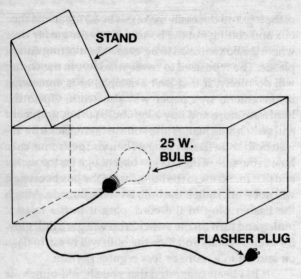

Figure 9

chapter? You are going to repeat that particular experiment, this time adding the teleflasher.

The initial work of this experiment is exactly the same as the one in the last chapter. You take a contact rate for your subject; find out by means of your pendulum when the target is sleeping, and at that time transmit your message. The difference in this particular working is that you are going to use the teleflasher to aid in the transmission.

It is of some importance to carefully choose the message which you will send. I have found that it is best to use a picture, preferably a photograph, to send to a sleeping subject, particularly if you are going to try to verify that the subject received your message without the subject knowing it. Let us assume for the moment that your subject is your long-suffering Aunt Mathilda. It would be a good idea to choose a picture that she would be likely to remember in the morning, say an old tintype of the ancestral mansion or something of personal importance to her. A photograph of yourself may be an excellent message, especially if she is going to visit you the next day. At the appointed time, she will be on the receiving end of a very potent telepathic transmission, so be certain you are sending something you really want her to receive.

When the time comes to transmit, have the box set up as in the first experiment of this type, at some place close at hand where you can lay your hand on the plate without being uncomfortable. You may even be able to rest the box on your lap, if that seems like the best way. Set the teleflasher on a table or desk so that the stand is about eye level. A number of large books can be used to elevate it. Prop the picture you are going to send against the stand on the teleflasher. When you turn on the flasher, you will immediately notice why this method of construction is better than the standard method. The light, coming up from the screen, will illuminate the front of the picture, whereas the standard method would leave the image in shadow.

It is not a good idea to completely darken the room you are working in. Remember what I said about the flashing light and your eyes. I have found that it is best to simply dim the room light slightly, or use a small lamp set at the other side of the room. It may take a few tests on your part to find what type of room lighting is best.

You are finally ready to begin. You sit before the flasher, lights dimmed, the box ready, your hand on the plate. Now get into a meditative state, as you have practiced. Get yourself good and relaxed, all concerns of the day banished from your mind. It is not necessary to focus your mind on the receiver for this. The box does that for you. Remember, once you put your hand on the plate, you are in contact with the subject. Turn on the flasher. Watch the image flash on and off, while keeping your mind as clear as possible. The flashing image will automatically be transmitted to Aunt

Mathilda, and she will have an exceptionally vivid dream about whatever picture you send. The next day, when she comes over for dinner, cunningly bring up a subject which will get her going on the dream you sent her, and watch as Uncle Harry becomes upset at his wife for talking about such nonsense during the football game.

I promised you I would explain how all this works and I got a little ahead of myself, but here is the why and wherefore.

I have already explained how the box locks on to a target subject, something like psychic radar aiming. The advantage of this is obvious. You do not have to concentrate on the target. The box does that for you. By making the connection between the box and yourself, you automatically lock in to the person to whom you are transmitting. This makes your sending much easier.

What goes on between the flasher and your hand is a little more complex. Working backwards, we know that one of the better emission points for psychic energy is the palm of the hand. When you lay your hand on the plate, you are hooking yourself into the circuit of the box, and whatever comes out of your hand is going to be shot at the target by way of the witness. As you are using the contact rate, this means that any energy you put out will be sent, no matter what form it takes or what information it contains.

The information comes from your brain, where whatever message you are sending is processed and usually mixed up with a whole bunch of other messages. This is one of the reasons why untrained senders have so much trouble getting results, and why I spent the beginning of this book teaching you how to concentrate on a single message or image.

The teleflasher makes that concentration easier, and were it not so difficult to do all the things that are necessary to make it work at the same time, the mind would be able to interface with the brain and send out the message on the flasher with little trouble. As it is, the combination of these devices creates a transmittal unit of great power and accuracy.

The eye, picking up the flashing light, sends the image to the brain, not in a steady flow, but in quick bursts. The more rhythmic the bursts, the more likely they are to activate that part of the brain which controls the sending of psychic impulses. Notice I said *brain* instead of *mind*. What we are working with here is nothing more than electrical activity, which in some unknown way causes the psychic capacity to become activated. If this were not the case, anyone could simply stare at a picture or word and transmit with the same accuracy as when the flasher is used.

As you have noticed, the key word in these experiments is *accuracy*. We are not going to be satisfied with vague impressions or parts of pictures that can pass for a church or chicken with equal facility. A tower, for example, can be the top of a skyscraper, or it can be a grain elevator. In the usual run of psychic experimentation, this sort of thing may be quite acceptable. After all, the last one hundred years have been spent trying to get people to realize that it is possible to see the tower at all and the amazement that this can be done was such that people neglected to look beyond it. For our purposes, however, these studies, especially now, have something quaint about them. After you have worked with radionics for any length of time, and in particular the material in this book, you will come to the feeling that the para-psychologists in their nice laboratories testing people in controlled environments and getting the same results that passed for parlor games in Victorian drawing rooms is somewhat akin to building a space ship for Mars while everyone else is trying to perfect the biplane. It is nice that they are still doing it, but we would hope that they would try to progress a little.

So let's get on with it. By now you know how to control what goes out of your mind when you transmit. Even if you have trouble holding an image, and some people do have a lot of trouble with that, the teleflasher solves that problem for you. You can lock on to a target with an accuracy that most missile designers would envy. So what are you going to do with this ability?

Theoretically, you should be able to send a message to *anyone, anywhere*, at any time. And send you can. The problems are at the receiving end. As we dis-cussed a long time ago, most people go through life with a lot of junk crowding their minds. That is why the experimenters in their laboratories go to so much trouble to block out any extraneous information coming in to their receivers. That is also why their experiments seem so primitive. We are simply working with a greater level of difficulty, and that's why there is so often a gap between theory and practice. In theory, for example, we know that you should be able to accom-plish anything in this book by simple meditation and visualization. In practice, that is not going to happen.

This is why you need these machines, and this is why you have to experiment with them; to find out what will work for you and what will not.

You learn this by the process of experimentation. And to properly perform an experiment, you have to know how to go about it. The ones I have given you are examples that have worked for me, but now you have to set out and create your own. I can, however, offer some advice on this.

Begin by choosing a subject whom you know. The time will come when you will be able to work with total strangers, but it is not good to start with them. By working with someone who is familiar, you are better able to verify your results, especially in light of requirement two. This requirement is that the person whom you are experimenting on has no idea that he or she is the subject of your work. This rule may strike a lot of people who work in this area as being unethical, but as you can guess by now, I am not overly concerned with other people's ethics. This rule will preclude one of the greatest problems involved in studying telepathy: namely expectations on the part of the receiver. You cannot have the problem of psi missing (which is when a test subject gets so many wrong answers that a reason has to be given) when the person on the receiving end does not even know that he is using his psychic receptors.

Try to get a good witness sample. If you have camera, good. If not, run out and buy one. Slides make the best witnesses because they solve the problem of what to do with the negative. Some radionic specialists insist on putting the negative into the witness can, while others insist that the negative should only be kept somewhere. By using slides, you can avoid this controversy altogether. Radionics can be confusing enough for the beginner without matters being made worse.

Do not expect miracles overnight. If you are trying to influence a dream, you can reasonably expect results the next day. If you are trying to influence attitudes or behavior, remember that many factors go into these things and you are only adding another, albeit a powerful one.

For example, your local politician is going to have to vote on a subject that you have some personal interest in; say a new tax on widgetmakers or something. You desire very strongly that this bill, like the enemy, shall not pass. Given the knowledge in this book, which you have diligently studied and put into practice at every conceivable opportunity, you make the quite reasonable decision to use the box and flasher. Now, if all things were to go according to the ideal, the politician would be properly influenced and vote against the bill with little effort on your part. But the world does not work on the basis of the ideal. In fact, it usually does its best to work in the contrary fashion. The politician has other influences working on him. The franistat makers are not only lobbying heavily, but there are more of them and they have donated considerable money to his campaign, to say nothing of the extra business they have given his wife's law firm. The politician himself has had some rather unfortunate experiences with widgets, one of which blew up in his face when he was but a boy, thus he views widgetmakers with something of the same disdain that yuppies feel towards steelworkers.

In the face of this overwhelming energy, you are going to sally forth and try to cause the politician to vote your way. It is quite possible that you may succeed, but it is not likely. It is, therefore, a good idea to know your target subject and be as familiar as possible with his general attitudes. It is, of course, possible to change attitudes, and I will explain why in some greater detail later, but at this stage of your practice it is best to work with the general pattern of your subject's view of the world than to try and change it.

You should always set up an experiment in such a manner that success is easily determined. In most books on psychic development, it is recommended that you try to make complete strangers turn around and look at you. This experiment is considered excellent because the stranger has, given normal behavior on your part, no reason to turn and look at you, and by turning he is verifying the results of the experiment. Try to create experiments in which the results are usually as obvious. It will make life much easier for you. As you go along, of course, you will want to experiment with matters of greater complexity and you should do so, but always remember never to make things more complicated than they already are.

End of sermon on experimentation. If you have been using the teleflasher with the box, you will notice that sitting with the box on your lap can be just a bit inconvenient, especially if you are put together like I am, and the thing keeps wanting to slide off. Well, take heart, because now I am going to describe a device that will make direct connections between yourself and the box much easier.

But first I have to digress a little. This next instrument is based on a gadget called the 'Magnetron.' The magnetron was originally a large vacuum tube used in the early days of television for the emission of microwaves. It has since been supplanted by another mysterious device called a klystrom, but back in the mid-1950's the magnetron was a necessary thing to have. It was so necessary that a French radiesthesist found himself with an idea (perhaps inspiration would be a better term). He discovered that the pattern of the tube when drawn on a piece of paper caused his pendulum to behave strangely. Putting a witness sample of a person in the center of the drawing caused the person who belonged to the witness to become energized.*

This instrument was adopted by Dr. Christopher Hills with certain modifications. He placed the pattern on a block of wood and surrounded the center of the pattern with eight small magnets, alternating their polarity. He discovered that this arrangement significantly increased the power of the device. He then proceeded to publish photographs of the device along with his explanation of how it works (never a good idea if you are in the business of selling these instruments, because it becomes very tempting for do-it-yourself mad scientists like myself to simply build our own versions). You guessed it. That is exactly what I did. I also made a few modifications of my own and the completed instrument, viewed from the top, looks

---

*Victor R. Beasley, *Your Electro-Vibratory Body*, (Boulder Creek, Calif.: University of the Trees Press, 1979), p. 47.

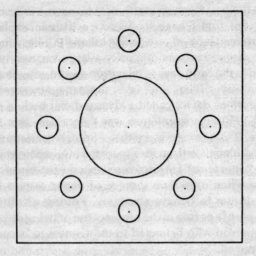

Figure 10

something like figure 10. Essentially, I made three changes. I retained the basic form of the large, white center circle surrounded by eight smaller circles, but eliminated the connecting lines between the center and the other circles. Instead of a block of wood, I glued the pattern to the top of a flat box and in place of the small magnets set into the smaller circles, I used a magnet strip of alternating polarities under the circles, glued in place to the underside of the box.

Aside from this description, however, I am not going to go into great detail about the Magnetron in use. It is primarily a healing device, with some potential as a psychic communicator. The University of the Trees, Hills' organization, has published a number of very good books in which the Magnetron is described in detail. I have only included it as a way of explaining the workings of my next device, the Psionic Amplifier Helmet.

The concept if a psychic amplifier built into a helmet is hardly original. Science fiction writers have played with it for decades. There was even a rather bad Boris Karloff movie, *The Devil Commands*, based on the idea. The most recent popular manifestation of the notion that putting something on your head would increase your psychic output appeared about ten years ago when some wag came up with the idea of a pyramid hat, to be worn while meditating, or out on the street for that matter. Fortunately, that particular notion died a most deserved death. Not only would a person look like a damned fool wearing a pyramid on his head, he would be running something of a risk as well. If a pyramid would mummify meat, think of what it would do to the human brain. When one thinks that 98% of the population has brains which are in less than perfect working order to begin with, the idea of them being made even worse is nothing less than terrifying.

Fortunately for all of us, my creation has none of those drawbacks. It stimulates the brain without damaging it, and, given the sort of things coming onto the market every day, can even be worn in public without anyone suspecting that it is not just a strange radio.

As you can see from figures 11 and 12, the component parts are built into the helmet itself, with the tuning dials at the front and the antenna encased in the crest. To build it you will need a plastic helmet, a hard hat will do very nicely, three variable capacitors, or condensers, otherwise known as radio tuning things,* a small jack, eight one-inch long pieces of magnet strip (available in dime stores, usually in the craft section) a piece of foil and wire, several feet of unshielded wire for the coil and antenna, and shielded wire for the other connections. You will also need a sheet of ½ inch Styrofoam and some duct tape. It is very important that you use a plastic helmet in making this device. A metal one will cause all types of difficulties and probably will not work at all.

The very first thing that you must do when you get the helmet home from the helmet store is try it on. This may sound silly, but I am assuming that you are using a plastic hard hat with the usual adjustable liner. It is important that this liner be adjusted to fit comfortably before you begin work, otherwise you may find yourself with wire connections that are too short, and some extra work that is easily avoided. Once you have the size right, put the helmet on and look in a mirror. Try to get some idea of how the project will look after it is completed. This is not a waste of time! A little thinking saves a lot of trouble.

Okay, now that you have an idea of what you are going to do, take the helmet off and look at the front. Find the center of the forehead, high enough so that the works of the condenser will be totally inside the helmet with the dial able to turn on the front freely without scraping the brim. Mark this point with a felt pen. Now measure a couple of inches off to each side of

---

*Potentiometers will work just as well.

this point and mark again, so that when the condensers are mounted, they will form a row in the front of the helmet with one at center and the other two at equal distances on each side.

At this point you should decide where you are going to put the jack. In my illustrations, I have placed the jack in the center at the back of the head, but you may wish to have it at one side. That's fine, but you have to remember that you have the part of the jack which is inside the helmet to deal with, and you don't want it scraping against your scalp or cheek. Once you have made up your mind on this, mark the spot on the outside of the helmet with the felt pen.

The last thing you have to mark is the center of the top of the helmet. Do this. That is the point where the antenna wire will come out.

Now that you have marked the appropriate points, take the helmet out to the garage and hook up your drill. But before you make any holes, be sure to measure the condenser stems and nuts, and the jack stem and nut because you will want to use the proper size drill. If the liner comes out, it is best to remove it before drilling. I realize that these instructions may seem elementary, but I have found from bad personal experience that the desire to finish a project has caused me to make some very stupid mistakes, and I would spare you that annoyance.

After you have drilled the holes, wire the three condensers in series the same way you wired the potentiometers in your box. Once you have done this, mount them on the helmet.

Take the magnet strip and cut eight one-inch strips.

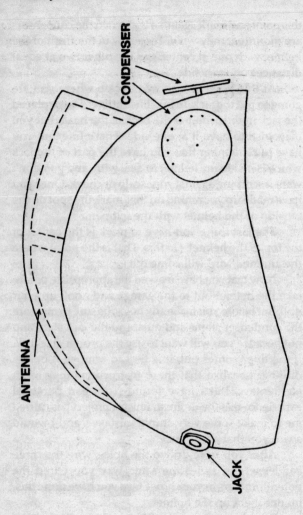

Figure 11

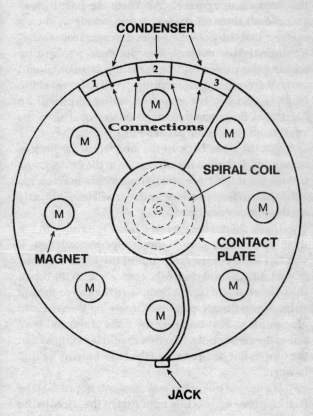

Figure 12

These are to be stuck on the inside of the helmet like the magnets in figure 12. Alternate the polarities as you mount them. A magnet strip is made in such a manner that the polarity is a bit different from that of an ordinary bar magnet. This problem is solved by sticking the pieces on in alternating horizontal and vertical arrangements. For example, if the strip at the front is vertical, the strips on either side will be horizontal. Be certain that the strips are equal distances apart from the center of each strip.

Put the liner back in the helmet, if the liner is removable. If there is no liner, go on to the next section. Cut the foil into a circle about three inches in diameter. Affix this circle to the liner so that it will press directly on the top of your head.

If you do not have a liner, make the coil with the unshielded wire, saving enough for the antenna. If you have not cut the circle out of the foil, do it now.

Mount the coil under the center hole in the top of the helmet. If you have a liner, wire the coil to the foil circle. If you do not, place the circle over the wire and glue in place, first bringing the ends of the coil wire out of the center hole. In either case, it is essential that the top of your head press on the foil when the helmet is worn.

It's time to put in the jack. You will notice that the jack has three connecting tabs. Attach the wires to the two outside tabs and ignore the center one. Making sure that the wires from the jack are long enough so they won't interfere with your head, attach the other ends of the wire to the foil circle with a drop of solder. Wire the condensers to the circle as in figure 12.

The inside of your helmet should now look pretty much like figure 12. It is only left for you to make the crest and antenna.

The antenna is only a length of wire that is encased in the crest. Make the crest first.

Making the crest is a little complicated, so pay close attention. Begin by cutting the sheet of Styrofoam into two equal pieces. Put them aside for a moment and proceed to make a pattern. You do this by taking a sheet of paper and taping it down to a table. Rest the helmet on its side on the paper, holding it so that the top of the helmet is parallel to the paper. Trace the curve of the helmet on the paper and then set the helmet to one side. Lift the paper from the table, being careful not to tear it and cut out the curved section where the helmet had been. Test your pattern by holding the paper along the top of the helmet. The curve cut out of the paper should fit the curve at the top of the helmet. If it does not, try again, and keep trying until it is right. This is very frustrating but also very important. The crest must fit properly.

Once you have the pattern fitted right, draw the complete crest on it. It should look just like the crest on the helmet in figure 11. Cut each piece of Styrofoam so that it fits the pattern and try each piece on the helmet.

Cut the wire for the antenna and lay it along the side of one of the pieces of crest. Be certain that the ends of the wire come out from under the crest. Spread glue on this and lay the other half of the crest over it. Now put a book on the arrangement and let it harden. If the helmet has a liner, attach the wires from the crest to the circle. If there is no liner, take the wires coming out of the top of the helmet and twist them to the wires of the antenna. After you have made this last connection, glue the crest to the top of the helmet so the completed helmet will look something like figure 11. All you have to do now, if you want to, is wrap the crest in duct tape, neatly, to protect the Styrofoam. If you wish to paint the completed helmet, and you may want to for the sake of appearance, it is best to paint it red. In fact, if the helmet is originally yellow, that may be a very good thing to do. Doctor Abrams, in the course of his experiments, made the surprising discovery that wearing red on the head increased psychic output, while yellow actually decreased it. There are certain obvious implications in such discoveries but I would never be so crass as to mention them. You should be able to figure that out for yourself.

At this point, you are probably wondering what use this marvelous instrument may have. Like all radionic instruments, the helmet has the capacity to tune and target psychic energy, in particular the energy that is emitted and received from the eyes. If you will remember from the beginning of this volume, the eyes are among the principal emission points for psycho-tronic power, and this has been proven by our little experiment with the straw revolving on the needle. The helmet will also increase the output of visualized energy and aid in the accuracy of any transmission with or without the teleflasher. By using a pendulum and numbered scale, I have discovered that my own output is increased by ten percent over normal while using the helmet. This is untuned energy. Targeted transmissions are correspondingly improved.

"Wonderful," I can hear you saying, "but how do I tune this miraculous device?" There are two ways to tune this instrument. The first method involves the use of the pendulum. Put the helmet on your head with the three dials turned to their lowest frequencies. Sit facing north. Facing north or south is of some importance which I will explain later. Holding your pendulum, begin to concentrate on somebody you know. As you concentrate, reach up with your left hand and begin to tune the knob at the left. Turn this knob very slowly until the pendulum begins to give a strong swing. Repeat this process with the other two dials. The reading on the dials is considered a rate, just as in using the box. You are now in telepathic contact with the person you were concentrating on and may prove it by sending him a message.

You are probably familiar with the usual instructions given in every book on psychic power. They all tell you to *see* the person you are sending to in your mind, and then transmit your message. I have given you the same instructions myself. What they do not tell you is that it's very important to keep your message as simple as possible. If you can break it down to one word or phrase, so much the better. In short, you send the same type of message you would send using the teleflasher, but without the benefit of that device. Why? Because when you do use the flasher in conjunction with the helmet, as you have used it with the box, it will be that much easier to determine if the teleflasher is helping your results.

There is an even better way to tune your helmet

than the pendulum. If you have been using the pendulum regularly, you will notice that it sometimes has the exasperating habit of giving false swings. These are minor gyrations that sometimes are all too easy to mistake for the real answer. When used in conjunction with the dials on your helmet, it can be positively infuriating.

I instructed you to install a jack on the back of the helmet wired to the central contact plate. Now you will learn why. One of the earliest gadgets, and one of the most useful, developed by George de la Warr, was the portable detector. It was, and still is, a rather cumbersome block of wood, hollowed out and fitted with a rubber stick plate on top. The hollow body is supposed to somehow increase the sensitivity of the item. Whether this is true or not, it does work. And now I have a bit of a confession to make. When I first built a radionics box, I had never heard of the portable detector. I had the little paperback in which de la Warr's work was discussed, but I had never paid much attention to it. So, to make my first machine simple, I created my own version of the portable unit and was quite proud of myself, thinking that I had made a new discovery. You can imagine my displeasure when I learned that the creation of which I was so proud had been invented by an eccentric Englishman some years before I was born! Oh well, they say humility is good for the soul.

Anyway, I will give you my design for the portable detector, rather than the de la Warr version, not only because it will greatly inflate my ego, but also because mine is a hell of a lot easier to make. What is needed is as follows: one (1) plastic stick plate, like the kind you put on your box; a length of unshielded wire; a length of speaker wire, about six feet should do; and a plug assembly such as one finds on earphones, the plug being the same type and size as the jack on the helmet. For example, if you used a ¼-inch mono jack, then you must use a ¼-inch mono plug. It is really quite simple. Take these items and figure 13 and get to work.

You begin by making a coil of the unshielded wire. You place this coil on the underside of the plate so that the coil is in the center and the two ends of the wire are extended near the edge of the plate. Tape this coil in place with electric tape.

Now strip the insulation off the ends of the speaker wire and separate the two strands. Do this at both ends. Twist one strand of speaker wire around one end of the coil wire and then repeat with the other strand. Wrap these connections with the electric tape.

Take the plug assembly apart. It should simply unscrew, leaving the plug and its connections on one piece and the shield (the little tube thing) as the other. Ideally there will be two small screws on the connectors of the plug. String the tube onto the speaker wire with the threaded end facing the end of the wire. If you do this wrong, you will have to redo the whole thing. Now attach the strands of speaker wire to the two connectors of the plug. Wrap a small piece of electric tape around the short connector and then screw the shield back onto the plug. Voila! You now have a portable detector just like the professionals use.

Now, what are we going to do with this miraculous

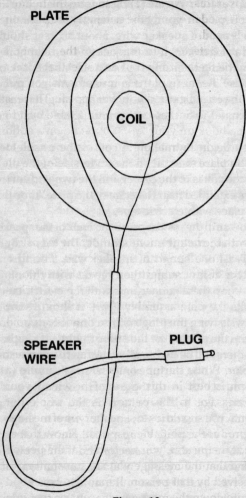

Figure 13

piece of apparatus? We are going to tune the helmet. This plate is used in exactly the same way the plate on your box is used.

Plug the detector into the jack of the helmet. I know you will feel a bit silly, but do not let that bother you, because the more of these instruments you put together, the less dignified you will appear. There is no way around it. Set the detector on a table next to you or on a book on your lap. It must be on a solid surface. Now concentrate on the person you wish to contact. While turning the dials on your helmet with your left hand, stroke the plate with your right thumb while bracing it with the other fingers. The stick will occur the same way as in the use of the box.

There are three principal experiments that you must do with the helmet alone, without the aid of any other apparatus other than the stick pad. The first, sending to a distant subject you have already done. The second experiment is much similar but requires the use of the detector and a witness sample. With the helmet on, lay the witness sample on the table in front of you and concentrate on the subject, while taking a rate on the helmet. Once you have the rate, disconnect the detector. While staring at the witness sample (a photograph is best in this experiment), send your thought-message to the person. As in our other experiments, you should try to send the type of message that will produce a verifiable response. Know that as you stare at the picture, you are staring at the person himself and that the message you are transmitting is being received by that person. It may also be a good idea to write down the message you sent, so that you will have a record to judge his response by.

As you can see, the first two experiments involved transmission of a message. The third requires you to be a receiver.

This can be just a bit risky. One of my more interesting experiments involved trying to help a friend who had just had root canal work done on one of her teeth (which is where it is usually done, so I am told). She was in some pain and I, being in a rare, generous mood, set up an experiment to help her. I had recently undergone a similar treatment, the result of which was that one of my front teeth was left hollow and filled with plaster. I was going to transmit the energies of the healed tooth to her empty one and thus cause her mouth to stop hurting. Simple, right? Well, it didn't turn out quite that way.

I placed the witness sample of myself in the can and set the rate, or what I *believed* to be the rate. I placed the picture of my friend at the other end of the circuit and let the arrangement sit. About a half hour later, I began to have pains in my tooth, which I knew had no nerve endings to have pain from. In short, I was experiencing the classic phantom pains, usually associated with amputees. This was most annoying, and, I will admit, a bit puzzling for a time. It did not, however, take me too long to discover what the problem was. I was getting a back-flow of energy from my friend. It later turned out that during the short time I was sending to her, her tooth had stopped hurting, but I had to take everything out of the system to stop my own jaw from paining me.

The conclusion I drew from this experience was

that by leaving a witness sample of myself, I had created a circuit which permitted the energies of her problem to enter my field. The circuit which should have only worked in one direction was operating in two.

In this experiment, the one you are going to try, you are going to be in direct contact with the energies of the person you are working with, and, unlike my tooth experiment, you are going to be wired to the subject, not merely your witness sample. So take a little care in the choice of your subject. Try to pick someone in reasonably good health and who is likely to be in a good mood at the time of your experiment.

So much for warnings. Now for the mechanics. Using the stick pad, take a rate for the person you are going to study. Once you have the contact rate, place the pad on the table in front of you. Now lay the witness sample on the pad, close your eyes, and see the person in your mind.

I can hear you saying "This just like psychometry!" Well, you are right, it *is* psychometry, but with an advantage. In ordinary psychometric work, the experimenter will just hold a witness and take what impressions he is lucky enough to get. Some people can become very adept at this and cause all manner of embarrassment to their friends. Me, I never could do it. If you handed me a ring belonging to a dwarf, I'd say that he was six-foot-eight with a wart on his nose. The machinery, with its targeting capacity, will enable you to zero in on your subject and be able to come up with things you never dreamt of, and quite possibly things your subject would rather you never had.

Let me give you an example. A friend of mine, let

us call him Orville (not his real name), was wondering whether he should invest his exhorbitant wages into a certain company. He had even gone so far as to have his broker send him a copy of the corporation's annual report. Now for those few of you who have never seen one, an annual report comes in a nice magazine format usually full of pretty pictures of the activities of the company and its officers. My friend read the report and thought it would be a good investment, but undoubtedly prompted by his guardian angel, decided to try my helmet and see if he could learn something else. He asked me if he could borrow mine, and I, owing him a favor, loaned it to him. It was probably one of the wiser things he has ever done. He cut out the picture of the company president and put it on the pad, after taking the rate. He closed his eyes and immediately saw the dread word "BANKRUPTCY" flash into his mind. It was quite a shock to him, so much so that he literally tore off the helmet. It was fortunate that I was right there or he might have damaged the delicate instrument. My friend decided at that point to put his money elsewhere, and two months later was gratified to learn that he had made the right decision. The company he was going to invest in had been forced to declare bankruptcy, and those who had seen their money go up with the rocket as its stock had increased in value a few months earlier now saw it come down with the stick.

I hope that by using the helmet to study people, you can have similar good fortune. But the helmet has another advantage. It can be hooked into your machine to give you greater accuracy.

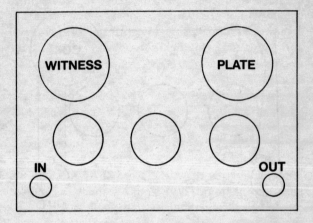

Figure 14

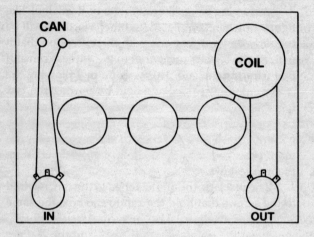

Figure 15

In order to do this, you are going to have to make a modification to your box, or better still, make a second one. I have a number of boxes myself and I have discovered that there are never enough of them available for the amount of work I have for them.

Assuming you make another box, it will look like figure 14 when completed. In other words, it will be the same as your first one with the exception that it will have two jacks, one wired to the witness can and one wired to the coil. This is done by following the diagram in figure 15. You begin by putting the box together in exactly the same way as your first one. Once you have completed that, punch a hole at the bottom of each corner. Take two jacks, preferably the same type you used in making your helmet. Wire them as follows.

The first jack, the one attached to the can, is wired to the screws that hold the can to the box, the same way the coil and the dial is. The second jack is wired to the coil at the points where the can and the dial are joined to the coil wire. Once you have attached the wire, push the jacks up through their holes and tighten the holding nuts.

Now that you have done this, get yourself to the local electronics store and buy a cable with a plug on each end, preferably of the same size as the jacks. If you get a different size you will have to buy adapters as well, and will come home feeling rather foolish about the whole thing. Once you are safely back in your workshop, set the box on a table and plug the wire into the jack on your helmet. The helmet is now connected to the box in the same way that your tape deck is connected to your stereo. By doing this, you have made it possible to work on a subject without having to hold the box, and you have also increased your accuracy. Remember, the more dials you have, the more accurate will be your instrument.

Now you must take a rate. One advantage to this arrangement is that you do not have to be wearing the helmet to get a rate on it. Simply put the witness in the can and take a rate on the box and the helmet in the same manner as you would with just the box alone. Once you have done this, it is quite easy to send a thought message to the subject.

With the box resting on the table, place the helmet on your head and face north or south. The reason for this is that the magnets arrayed inside the helmet create a field inside the head of the person wearing the helmet. It is not a particularly strong field, but it *is* sufficient to increase the output of that part of the brain which controls psychic activity. By aligning yourself north-south, you are lining up with the magnetic field of the earth itself and that alignment, added to the field inside the helmet already, increases the output of the device. It is all rather complicated, and, to be truthful, I doubt that anyone really understands what exactly is going on. The situation is something like the one for radionics, which, as I have already stated, has inspired as many explanations as there are practitioners. The results are what count, and the helmet can bring results.

Anyway, now that you have this thing on your head, you are going to have to work with it. The first thing you must do is stop laughing at yourself. I remember the first time I sat in this arrangement I thought to myself that now I knew how Julius Rosenberg must have felt. I know it feels silly, and it looks silly as well. I'm afraid that there is no way to look dignified while sitting with a strange helmet on your head which is plugged into a cardboard box. The first thing you have to do is stop feeling so self-conscious! It might, however, be a good idea not to let anyone else see you at this point, because even if you can stop yourself from giggling, I can guarantee that anyone else will go into hysterics.

Now that you have a rate and have calmed down, begin to concentrate on the message, just as you have done with the helmet before. If you have chosen your subject and your message properly, you should be able to judge the results in the usual manner.

The same procedure is followed in remote viewing experiments. The only difference is that you will plug the helmet into the jack wired to the stick pad *after* you take your rate. This action will tell your subconscious mind that you are going to be *receiving* impressions rather than *sending* them. Other than that, you experiment with this in the same way as you did with just the detector. You should, however, notice that your reception is much sharper. Perform this experiment a number of times, the more the better. It may be a good idea to use a tape recorder while you are doing this, so that you can record your impressions.

Once you have tried your hand at remote viewing, you can add the teleflasher to your experiments. Again, the important thing to remember is that your results must be easily verifiable. A repeat of the dream experiment with your aunt Mathilda might be a good one to start with, inasmuch as you are already familiar with the probable results with that individual. Or you might like to try something a little more adventurous. In that case, the politician experiment is an excellent test of your skills.

The addition of the teleflasher to your array of equipment is really quite simple. The only problem you may face is a need for more space and a guarantee of privacy while you work.

You arrange your equipment as before; the box on a table next to you and the helmet on your head. You must then place the teleflasher in such a position that you can look at it without the wires from the helmet getting in the way. Never forget that when using the teleflasher you must keep all visual distractions to the barest minimum. You would be amazed at how annoying the slightest shadow over the image can become, and the sensitivity of the equipment you are now using is such that any emotion that you feel will be transmitted along with the message. You do not want your subject to pick up any feelings of frustration or anger along with your message. For him to do so would only detract from your results.

But the teleflasher can be used in much more subtle ways than the mere sending of a message to your subject. Let us assume that you are totally enamored of another person and you wish to make her (or him) notice you. Thus far, all of your efforts, including thought-forms, meditation, even the use of the box have proved failures. The combination of all of the above elements can greatly increase your effectiveness in dealing with this problem.

Let us assume you have already done your preliminary work. You have acquired a witness of the person in question, at least her name, and have prepared your box and helmet by finding the contact rate for this individual. Good. Now you must proceed as you did with the dream experiment, only in this case you are going to place the image of yourself in the mind of that person.

This is really very easy. Once you have determined by means of your pendulum when your target is likely to be asleep, set up your equipment. The image you will transmit, however, is a photograph of yourself, preferably in some pose your target will find pleasing. Know that as you prepare to transmit, your target is locked into your equipment and anything

you send is going to quite literally blast its way into her subconscious. With that knowledge in mind, take a few minutes to meditate and prepare yourself for sending. When you feel that you are calmed down and ready, turn on the flasher and open fire. I mean that last phrase quite literally. Each time the flasher lights, your mind is going to be sending the image of yourself like a psychic cannon shot at your subject. There is not a single thing that she can do to resist it. And this is why you work when your target is sleeping. If the subject is awake, she might be too busy, too pre-occupied to let your message through. Or she may receive it and have it burst into her conscious mind only to be instantly dismissed. But if she is sleeping, her defenses are down and her subconscious is wide open. There is only one defense against this form of transmission and it is unlikely that she will know it, so you are home free, as far as placing the picture of yourself in her mind. Now the question becomes one of what you are going to do with that picture.

After several nightly treatments with the machine, you should notice your subject is responding to you much differently from before. She will at least be noticing you. But you do not want it to stop there. So now you have to add something to the image.

At this point I am going to assume that you want to do something more with this person than sit and talk. You may have even gotten to that stage if you are lucky. In any event, you would like a little bit of lust to be present in the relationship. This can be accomplished with some extra work; the extra work in question being the acquiring of an appropriately erotic photograph of a couple thoroughly and physically enjoying each other. Once you have done this, you must increase your transmittal time. For example, let us assume that you transmit at one in the morning for five minutes. Continue this, but now transmit the picture of yourself for two minutes, the picture of the couple for two minutes, and then the picture of yourself again. Once you have done this for a few evenings you should notice some results, but they are going to be up to you. Wars have been lost by generals unwilling to exploit a breakthrough.

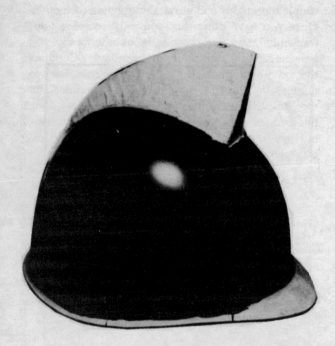

This is a simpler version of the Psionic Amplifier Helmet. Unlike the one described in the text, it is tuned by simply facing north. It is wired the same way that the one in the text is, minus the tuning dials. The advantage to this design is a little less weight. It does not, however, have the accuracy of the tuned helmet.

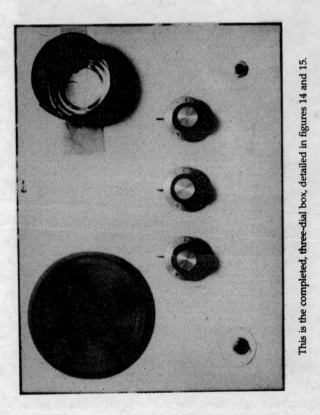

This is the completed, three-dial box, detailed in figures 14 and 15.

This box is a bit different from the ones I explain, but it operates in much the same manner. The metal plates are foil and the witness sample is held down by a rubber band stretched between two paper fasteners. You notice that the portable detector is attached to the box on the left, rather than the right side. That is due to a slight mistake I made while putting the wiring in, but the box works just the same.

9

Meet Other Minds

This chapter may seem a bit like a journey into outer strangeness, but I am quite serious. The machines you have built can be of great use to you in gathering much useful information from any human source, and the source does not even have to be living to give it to you.

By now, you have already used your pendulum to learn various things which would not be apparent to you if you did not have it. You have also conducted remote viewing experiments with the box and helmet. In the performance of these experiments, you have probably discovered that there are a few unsatisfactory elements in your results. The pendulum will give incorrect answers if you are too emotionally involved in the question, and the remote viewing experiments will leave you with images that tend to be a bit too fleeting for proper interpretation.

If you are like me, you are likely to be less than satisfied with anything but concrete information that can be verified and then acted on. Sure, the pendulum and box help, but is there any way that they can be improved upon? Yes, there is and it is as simple as combining them.

Do you remember the technique I used to help my friend with his investment problem? Let us consider what went on when he put on the helmet and got the impression that he did. The witness of the company president was the link between that individual and my friend. Because of that witness, my friend was able to make a working link between his conscious mind and the subconscious mind of the subject. The possibility of bankruptcy was very strong in the mind of the subject, so strong that the moment the link was established, the word blazed into the mind of my friend. It was very simple and direct.

But let us suppose that we are dealing with matters that are not so pressing. The emotional content may be a bit muddled or completely lacking. There may be nothing present that will immediately show itself, and thus nothing will come through but the vague impressions and images that are the base of every psychic. By combining the targeting capacity of the box with the concrete responses of the pendulum, that problem can be largely eliminated.

Let me give an example. Another friend of mine, let us call her Miss Z., needed to find a document that had been put aside by one of her employees. Now under normal circumstances it would have been a simple matter for her to get the employee on the phone and ask her where the document was. There was only one problem. The person in question was on vacation somewhere in the Ozarks and nobody knew exactly where. To make matters worse, it was doubtful that even if the employee could be found, she would be nowhere near a phone. I, on the other hand, was readily available.

As I was eating lunch, my phone rang, with Miss Z. on the other end, frantic to the point of incoherence. After much coaching, she finally calmed down enough to tell me the problem and ask if I could do my strange stuff and find the document. Now this is a bit of a problem, you must admit. It just is not done, walking around an office with a pendulum looking for lost papers. Sure, I did it when I was working for my father, but everyone knew me and I could get away with it. This environment was not going to be so friendly. I told Miss Z. to calm down and I would be over as soon as I could.

I packed my helmet and box into a case and went to her office, where I was ushered into the most private room we could find. After all, if someone came in and saw what we were doing, it would have been a bit embarrassing. Well, it was a bit of a shock for my friend when I set up to work. She had heard me talk about my interests and had even seen me do a few small demonstrations with the box and even the pendulum, but the helmet wired into the box was just a bit much even for her. In fact, she almost forgot her problem trying to keep from laughing. I told her I knew it looked ridiculous but that she had to stay calm and get me a picture or something of the employee. She ran out to get the needed items while I sat there thinking that I was never going to live this down. Miss Z. came back in a few seconds, making sure that the door was closed behind her.

With the picture in the box, I took a rate just as I

have described in this book, both on the box and on the helmet. Then I did something that nearly gave Miss Z. a heart attack. I told her to put the helmet on and try to contact her employee. She did not seem too enthusiastic about the idea, but *she* knew what she needed, and I, who know nothing of the mysteries of office management, had no idea. So Miss Z. donned the helmet and closed her eyes for a few seconds, opened them and told me that the fish were not biting. I buried my face in my hands and shook my head. It was definitely turning into one of *those* days. I took out my pendulum and chart, (you remember the chart I had you make in that chapter) and told her to hold the pendulum over the chart and ask where the document was. She was to forget about the fishing and concentrate on the document. In a matter of seconds, the pendulum began to swing, spelling out the location of the mysterious paper. It was in her desk, under a box of some personal items where she had put it during one of those hurried moments that occur at least once a day. Miss Z. ran out of the room and reappeared a minute later, waving the paper. I packed up and went home to a well-deserved nap.

I forgot the incident, but a couple of weeks later I got another call from Miss Z. It seemed that her employee told her that she had been fishing and while being frustrated at the lack of results, she suddenly found herself concentrating on the paper she had previously unceremoniously jammed into her desk and wondered if it was important. Well, after a few years, you get used to this sort of thing, but it is always something of a shock for a beginner.

Now why did we have to go through all this trouble? I have already said that the pendulum alone was not going to work. The pendulum and chart might have worked in a calmer environment. But my friend was anything but calm at the time, and pendulums have been known to lead people on merry chases when they get too involved with what they are looking for. The pendulum did it to me last week. I was sufficiently disinterested that I could have used the pendulum, but I had no concept of what was being searched for, and as far as I knew, one piece of paper was as good as any other. No, we had to be certain that the subject was providing the data. As you can tell from the immediate impression Miss Z. got, just asking the question, even with the box and helmet, was not going to be enough. But when the pendulum and the chart were combined with the box and the helmet, the desired information came through immediately and accurately.

So now we come to your own work with these devices. When you set up an experiment with this equipment, do it in the same manner as your remote viewing experiments from the last chapter. Once you have your rate, use the pendulum and chart as you did when I explained their use.

A good procedure to follow in this matter is to choose a subject that you know reasonably well, certainly well enough that you ask what he or she was doing at the time you perform the experiment. Once you have chosen your subject and taken the rate, ask the pendulum to describe for you *in detail* what your subject is doing at that time. As the words are spelled out, record your findings, and, assuming they are not going to embarrass your subject, ask that person the next day.

As you become skilled at this technique, you will be able to use it on people you don't know, but are nonetheless able to acquire a witness sample for. Politicians are excellent for these experiments for two reasons. First, they love nothing more than to have their pictures in the paper, so you can, with relatively little effort, acquire a photograph of one. Second, the politician is, by his very nature, prone to telling less than the whole truth. That is not to say he (or she) is lying, but merely that he is not giving out all the information available. With this mechanism, that trick can't work on you.

This method will differ somewhat from the lie detector experiments I had you perform in the previous chapters because you are less interested in whether or not an outright lie has been told than you are in getting the entire story. Hence, you will not ask if statement so and so is the truth. What you *will* ask is for the person being questioned to tell you the facts of the situation, such as his intention to vote on some issue that he has publicly spoken on, but spoken in less than forthright terms.

For example, you, for obvious reasons, want to know if your congressman plans to vote for a tax increase. Now he has been asked this many times, but has never given a clear answer on the matter, thus arousing your natural suspicions. An ordinary voter would have a problem at this point, because he would have no idea what his congressman has in mind. You, however, are no ordinary voter and your congressman's mind (assuming he has one) is open to you. You set up the machine as you always do, taking a contact rate for the representative. In this case all you want is a simple yes or no answer, "Mr. X, are you going to vote for a tax increase after you are elected?" Keep repeating the question until the pendulum gives you a response, either yes or no. Once you have this information, you can go into the voting booth and make an informed decision, without having to rely on the leavings of the local press.

As you can imagine, this equipment lends itself to all manner of possibilities, so I will give you a word of caution. Sometimes it is better not to know too much about your neighbors. It can become very tempting to spend all of your time eavesdropping on other people's thoughts, but it is not very wise. If you catch him at a bad moment, such as if you have just mowed your lawn and he is looking out his window thinking that now he has to mow *his* lawn and is not very happy about it, you may get an erroneous impression which can ruin a friendship; so take everything you get, particularly in your early experiments, with more than a grain of salt. Also, you must never forget that the machine is only as good as the operator. If you really believe something, the machine, even set up as I have described, will only confirm that belief. If you want to be reassured about something, this device will do just that, only the truth may be just the opposite. So be careful how you use this stuff.

So much for the mundane uses for the machine-pendulum combination. Now we take off into outer strangeness. Your machine can get you into contact with people who are still alive. It can also put you into contact with those who are dead.

These experiments present a number of problems. While the mechanics of them, taking the rate, witnesses, etc., are the same as interrogating the living, the problems are much different.

Your first difficulty is choosing a person to contact. Ideally, it will be someone for whom you can obtain a witness sample. This would seem to indicate that a dead relative or friend is the best subject. Not true. The one type of person you must avoid contact with is someone to whom you were close while that person was alive. It can be *very unhealthy* for you to get into close contact with the spirit of such a person. What you must do is pick a subject that you had no personal contact with at all.

Your second difficulty lies in verifying any information you may receive from this person. Accept the fact that much of what you are told cannot be verified and be willing to file it away as interesting information, but not absolutely useful, or even true for that matter.

The final thing to remember is that you are the one in control of the experiment. This is not like the usual stuff of sitting with a Ouija Board (which, incidentally, can be used in place of the pendulum and chart) and waiting for the message to come through from some unknown source. You already know who the source is, and ideally, enough about that source to know that something you are being told is not right. Control also means that you do not accept blindly any emotions or other feelings that come through while performing the experiment. If something doesn't feel right, end the experiment immediately. I cannot tell exactly what I mean by not 'feel right,' but you will know if it happens. It is nothing to worry about; your equipment can balance anything that is too out of the ordinary, but you must break contact at once.

So much for the difficulties. Let's assume that you have the witness sample and the rate and are beginning to get a response from the subject. It is a good idea to avoid specific questions. You should already know any specific information about his life that he might give you. It is far better to ask more general questions, such as the nature of his present environment; perhaps a description of the surrounding countryside. It is unwise to ask him anything about your own life. It is doubtful that your subject even knows who you are, and equally unlikely that he can give you any information that would be of value. It is proper to ask him about events in his life that you may be aware of, and, if you are lucky, some information may come through which can be verified by a little research. Sometimes such research is not necessary. Ex-politicians are a gold mine of hidden scandals that tend to come out years after they are dead. It may seem that I have a tendency to pick on political leaders in my research, and it isn't out of malice, but the fact remains that their witness samples are so easy to obtain (a newspaper photo will do) and that any data I come up with can be verified with little effort. I recommend you follow the same practice.

I have found that those I have contacted are usually very willing to help with specific problems. I know this seems to contradict what I have just said, but there are times when you may need some definite help on a specific matter. There is no harm, therefore, in using this technique to help yourself out of some difficulty.

Let us say, for example, that you are writing a novel and have managed to write yourself into a corner. This is a problem that occurs with unfortunate frequency to the best of us. In this situation, it is perfectly all right for you to take a witness of a famous writer who has recently departed this mortal coil and dial him up for some advice. The same can be true for the spirit of the local auto mechanic whose passing has left you with the problem of finding an honest replacement. Anyway, you get the idea.

There is only one caveat to using the machines in this manner. You have to be a little practical in what you ask. You are not likely to get the location of the

Lost Dutchman Gold Mine, so try to avoid that kind of nonsense. Of course, there is nothing to prevent you from asking a famous former horse breeder who he likes in the fifth, but do not bet the family home on the answer he gives you. Use a little common sense, as out of place as that commodity may seem in this matter.

In these next experiments, you may well think that all sense has flown to the four winds. You now know how to contact those who are living, and no longer living. Now you will learn how to contact those who may not even be *human*. If you do any work along this line, I would ask that you consider it to be purely in the nature of an experiment and not go hog wild over any information you may receive. Take any contact with a heavy dose of salt and try not to form a new religion.

There is a long-standing tradition that humans are not the only intelligent life forms inhabiting the unseen realms; that among the various creatures to be found there are gods, angels and various nature spirits that may disguise themselves as gods or angels. There is also a strong tradition which asserts that these beings have a certain love of playing pranks on long-suffering humans, particularly those who run into them without knowing the proper etiquette. So take the usual precautions before venturing into these realms, such as avoiding drugs and strong drink, and keep a tight hand on the helmet plug, in case you want to break contact in a hurry.

The cautions understood, you must realize that you will be flying blind, as it were. There are no witness samples for these beings, unless you wish to contact the spirit of a local tree. That happened to my mother by accident one night many years ago. She was lying in bed, looking out the open window with Father sound asleep next to her, and her state of mind was apparently so relaxed that she was somehow able to see into the astral realm. Next thing she knew, a man in a red suit with a copper thing on his head appeared to float towards the window, scaring her half to death, and she never looked at the tree across the street the same way again.

Anyway, as there are no witness samples, the technique you will use is a bit different. You will tune your box and helmet much as you would tune a radio when looking for a new station whose call letters you don't know. Plug the helmet into the box with all the helmet dials set at the maximum point, the highest frequency if it has tuning capacitors, ten if potentiometers. This will allow any signal from the box to come through unrefined by the tuning mechanism of the helmet. Set all three dials on the box to 0. Now, relax, close your eyes and think about what you want to contact. As you do this turn the left-hand dial of the box until you feel that you have hit the right point. You may also use the stick pad, as in taking a rate. This will give you the basic location of the subject, whatever that subject may be. Repeat the procedure with the next two dials. After you have done this, you should have a clear visual image in your mind of the subject. If you wish further refinement, you may use the dials on your helmet.

These instructions may seem a bit sketchy, but this procedure has a lot of trial and error, and there is no way to be more concrete. You must learn through experiment. But once you have made your contact, if you wish to engage in any conversation, it is best to open your eyes and use the pendulum, counting on your equipment to maintain the contact for you.

There is a risk in this that you should be made aware of, though not paranoid. Part of the traditional prankishness of some things floating around out there is a joy in taking control of the lives of those who are susceptible to them. Now by this I do not mean that you might find yourself spitting green glop at people and turning your head all the way around, but there is a slight risk in most people, and a serious risk in a few, of unpleasant and possibly dangerous side effects from such contact. While I have never seen it, the anecdotal evidence is convincing.

The best way to avoid such problems is to always remember that *you* are the one in control. As long as you keep that fact firmly in mind, you should have little trouble. Likewise, it is not a good idea to follow specific instructions given by such contacts. I am sure that you wouldn't be so foolish as to pay any attention if one told you to go out and murder your Aunt Mathilda. After all, who would you then have to experiment on? Even the most benign instructions must be given a good deal of thought before being acted upon. As in contacting the dead, do not go out and bet the family homestead on the horse just because the spirit says you would.

The same instructions apply to contacting extra-terrestrials. In fact, I wish that I did not even have to bring this subject up, but there is so much nonsense going around that I, knowing that some of my readers will not be able to resist trying, have to say something on the matter.

In this the greatest danger is that of an over-active imagination. The experimenter may wish to make contact with such fervor that he is unable to avoid letting that desire determine his results. In effect, he is contacting his own subconscious and will hear exactly what he intends to. Sometimes this is harmless, other times the person goes out, buys a purple robe and convinces various brainless movie stars that the science-fiction voice is that of an "enlightened" being from another world.

Assuming that you are able to avoid the pitfalls of this, you will find the experiment to be fascinating one. Just be sure to keep your skeptic hat firmly on and never forget that there is a world of difference between having an open mind and an empty head.

10

Power Merge

Congratulations again! You have made it to the final chapter and now you are going to learn how to put everything you have learned to use at the same time.

Ready?

Here we go.

First we need a hypothetical situation. Let's take something common, like job hunting.

In order to get the job you want, you must first find a place that wants your skills. We will assume here that you already know what those are. Not only must the company want your skills, it must also want you.

Back to finding the place to work for. You have searched the want ads daily and diligently, and, despite your best efforts, have found nobody advertising for the type of work you do best. Now is the time to start making thought-forms. Create your first thought-form as you learned so long ago and send it forth with the instructions to create a number of openings in your field. That is all you want this thought-form to do.

While you are waiting for that thought-form to

work, begin working on yourself. Use the money-attracting techniques you were taught and begin to condition your energy field to attract people to you, to make them like you. This is very important. Continue to work on yourself and send forth thought-forms about openings until an opening occurs.

When you see the ad for the job you want, ask the pendulum if this is right for you. The pendulum will probably say yes because of your emotional involvement with the answer, but that is all right at this point because you need confidence, and if it is really terribly wrong for you, you might get a warning.

Now is the time to bring up the machine. Let's assume that the advertisement has a number to call for an interview appointment. You will call the number and make an appointment for several days hence. There usually is a short waiting time in any job worth having. Use that time.

Immediately after you make the appointment get a witness sample of the place where you are going to be interviewed. All you need is a photograph of the outside of the building. Time is important, so try to use an instant camera for this. Return to your home immediately and put the picture in the machine and get a contact rate for the building.

Ideally, you should have the name of the person you are appointed to meet with. It is probably a good idea to ask for that name if you can do it without sounding odd. It is not necessary to get the spelling right, because all you want is a focusing point for what comes next.

You have the picture and the name in the box.

The box is tuned to the contact rate for the company. Now take a rate on your helmet. Once you have that, you are ready to go on to the next steps.

With the helmet on, try to see the office in the building where you will be interviewed. Try to get as clear an image as possible, but don't worry if it fades in and out a bit. They usually do. It is sufficient to know that your mind is linked to the environment of that office.

Once you have placed your psychic body into the office, you must create a thought-form. You do this just as you did in that chapter when I taught you how to make a thought-form that would influence an entire room. You create this thought-form with the instruction that anyone entering that office will be filled with an intense liking for you, and no one who comes into contact with it will be able to resist the warmth of your scintillating and dynamic personality.

This should be enough in most cases to help anybody, but we are not through yet. Now we go after the person who does the hiring.

Remove the picture of the building from the machine and take a new rate, this one for the individual who is conducting the interview. As I have taught you, use the pendulum to find out when he is going to be sleeping. At that time, set up a smiling, happy picture of yourself on the teleflasher and send that picture to him. Now, using a heavy magic marker, write the word "HIRE" on a small piece of paper and send that word to him. Follow that with another dose of your picture.

If you perform all of these activities with diligence,

you should merely have to walk into the office to be given the job. It is a rare individual indeed who can resist the power of this type of bombardment.

The important things to remember when you combine your techniques and equipment are that you should know what you want and be willing to do what is necessary to get it. Do you remember my opening comments on power? Well, now you have it and it is important, vitally important, for you to remember that power exists to be used, without hesitation and without remorse. You have a lot of stuff available now. Use it.

Let's try something else. There is a cute girl who works in the public library and you would like to get to know her. The only problem is that you are scared silly. The usual pick-up methods either don't work for you, or you lack the type of nerve necessary to use them. (Women, this technique will work the same on men.)

You begin by doing a little homework. Try to find out her name, at least her first one. This is not as difficult as it may seem. All you have to do is keep your ears open. Someone is bound to ask her by name for something. Once you have that piece of information, you can proceed in much the same manner as you did when seeking employment.

Meditate and try to visualize the interior of the library. Once you have that image, create a psychic land mine over the place most likely to be crossed by your subject, such as the main desk or the front door. The purpose of this thought-form is going to be simply creating a great liking for you in anyone who runs into it, nothing more. Work on this thought-form for some time until you know it's broadcasting with some strength. If you have any trouble with the visualization, get a picture of the library building and proceed as I instructed in the section on job hunting.

After you have done this, you must create another thought-form, this one aimed directly at the subject. You will instruct this one to soften her up, as it were, so that she will be receptive to you and your transmissions. Make this thought-form as powerful as you can and send it on its way.

Now set up your box with a contact rate for the subject. The night before you are planning to go to the library, transmit a photograph of yourself to the subject. We have already discussed this procedure in some detail, so you should know how to do it. All that remains is for you to work on yourself a little.

Build a thought-form in your own energy body which will cause people to be attracted to you. Continue to work on this, while you are doing the other parts of this experiment. In particular, work on your self-confidence, because no matter how much energy you put into the bombardment, the time will come when you will have to bite the bullet and introduce yourself. Of course, if you have an extremely receptive subject, she might make the first move.

Now that you have fortified yourself and your position, attack (not literally). Walk into the library expecting results and do not be too surprised when they occur.

The above techniques can be adapted to every-thing from selling vacuum cleaners to getting rid of noisy neighbors. All you have to do is decide which methods are best and then combine them as seems necessary. The purists out there would object that by doing this you may not know for sure which technique was the deciding factor, but we are not interested in that. What we want are results and this method brings them.

So there you have it. The course was not too difficult, was it? By now you are already discovering you can do things you never seriously thought you could, and I would hope that life is beginning to bend your way a little more. Above all, never stop trying, even if one technique or another seems a little difficult to master. After all, you are not trying to sink submarines or conquer gravity. Leave that sort of thing to the miracle mongers. And if the machines seem a little primitive, do not be afraid to add something of your own. I have tried to keep things as simple and inexpensive (downright cheap, actually) as possible. This is something new, less than a century old, and there is much to learn about it. The nature of the study is such that the hobbyist in his garage has as much chance of making a breakthrough as the researcher in his expensive laboratory. In the realm of psychism, even high-tech psychism, the results come not from the equipment so much as the person using it.

And with that I will end my babbling. What comes now is truly up to you.

APPENDIX

As you should be able to guess, the material included in this book is pretty powerful stuff. I have tried to make it as simple as possible so that just about anyone can master the techniques and devices in the book. The exercises were also designed to help the beginner over the usual difficulties which bedevil most people when they start with psychic powers. They are the methods which I have found to be the most effective in my years (almost 26) of studying and practice. Now, it is possible that a certain exercise or method may not quite set with the ethical views of certain readers. We all make our own decisions in such matters and none of us are in a position to decree what is right or wrong for another. If you should run into such a problem where a particular exercise conflicts with your personal beliefs, by all means do not use it. By the same token, I would hope that the ethical system which you base that decision upon is your own and not merely the views imposed by another.

There is one area that I did not cover in this work as it seems a little out of place in a book intended for beginners, and that is the subject of psychic combat. Nevertheless, it may at some time be necessary for you to protect yourself in a situation of extreme emotional negativity where your ability to function might be damaged. I do not ascribe to the point of view that we are endangered by the negative thoughts of everyone who dislikes us. If I thought that, I would be in real trouble. No, this exercise is only for those special occasions of real difficulty, such as when driving on a crowded highway, surrounded by the thoughts of lunatics whose only purpose in life is to get from one place to another on time, or any situation where you feel that you may be the subject of unwanted psychic transmission. It will not stop a determined attack, and that type of problem will be discussed in my forthcoming book *Psionic Power*, but it will help you through most difficulties.

Meditate and visualize yourself surrounded by a field of glowing, white light. Know that this light is a shield which will block any detrimental psychic influence. See this field glowing very brightly and say to yourself "I am surrounded by an impenetrable field of power. No enemy can injure me. The power fills me and enfolds me, and no evil can approach me."

The use of this exercise on a regular basis will give you all the protection anyone should normally need.

A Note From the Publisher

In publishing this second edition in mass-market format, I considered very carefully some of the criticism that was directed against publication of the first edition.

In general this criticism followed two lines of thought:

1. The techniques in the book are too dangerous to be given to the general public, especially when many of the examples given in the text tended to be "negative," i.e. involving things like *psychic projectiles* aimed at the back of an unaware person's head.

2. That the book isn't *New Age* in the sense that the author shows that these techniques can be used for the manipulation and even control of other people.

Well, in general, there's truth to these criticisms. But, the real truth is that we are dealing with the author's *style* on the one hand, and on the other hand with recognition that the psychic world we live in is filled with continued efforts at mind control and emotional manipulation, with negative thought-forms and projectiles, and more.

It's just the way it is, and the more the general public knows about this, the better off they are! If you didn't believe in germs and disease bacteria, you wouldn't exercise much common sense about personal cleanliness or the condition of the food you eat. If you didn't presume that the sales person offering you a wonderful deal over the telephone had ulterior motives, you wouldn't be as cautious in determining your appropriate response to those solicitations.

The psychic world is *real!* Every politician seeking your vote is projecting psychic images as well as the emotion-laden words he speaks as he attempts to manipulate your behavior. Every person with whom you are in contact is radiating psychic energies and forms that impinge upon you, and many of them are working to influence what you do. Every time someone attempts to influence you with words, they are—to greater or lesser degrees—also using psychic techniques, whether they know it or not. That's because we are psychic beings just as much as we are physical, mental and spiritual beings.

With this awareness, you have every reason to be as conscious of the psychic world as you are of the physical. Learn to strengthen your aura with the simple technique of the white light shield described by the author in the Appendix. I also recommend *The Llewellyn Practical Guide to Psychic Self-Defense* which expands upon these concepts and gives detailed exercises for building your psychic strength.

The author's style is effective in getting your attention, and his examples and suggested experiments are effective in getting these ideas across. Just because he describes using a "psychic drill" doesn't mean that such a psychic drill actually is the same *dangerous* tool that a physical drill is. Psychic images are not the same as their physical counterparts, as you will learn. The electric drill is just an image with which you are familiar, and is one that helps focus your psychic energies sufficiently to make the experiment a success.

Do you have the right to use your psychic powers in such a negative fashion, merely for amusement or experimentation?

That's a question only you can answer. We don't impose our ethical standards on your behavior. But, I do have a fundamental belief that once you perceive that your willed images do have power, once you are aware of their reality, you will be as careful and considerate in recognizing your psychic strengths as you are your physical strengths. We don't worry about the casual "blow" delivered to our face by the waving arms of a small baby—and right now you are not much more than an infant in terms of your psychic development. However, with awareness and with exercise, those skills and powers will grow—and with their development comes responsibility.

We evolve through the awareness of and acceptance of our responsibilities. *And continued evolution is the only logical justification I have ever found for us to be here in the first place!* We don't live in a perfect world, but we should keep on trying to make it so.

We do not grow and evolve through ignorance. Keeping knowledge from people deemed "unworthy" is the old argument used in defense of an elitist society.

The real challenge is to you, dear reader, now that you have read this book, to get busy and develop your psychic skills and extend your awareness of the world about you based on these new perceptions.

Carl Llewellyn Weschcke

Select Bibliography

Allen, Phil; Bearne, Alastair; and Smith, Roger. *Energy, Matter and Form*. Boulder Creek, Calif.: University of the Trees Press, 1979.

Bardon, Franz. *Initiation Into Hermetics*. Wuppertal, West Germany: Dieter Ruggeberg, 1971.

Beasley, Victor R. *Your Electro-Vibratory Body*. Boulder Creek, Calif: University of the Trees Press, 1979.

Denning, Melita and Phillips, Osborne. *The Llewellyn Practical Guide to Creative Visualization*. St. Paul: Llewellyn Publications, 1980.

Dublin, Reese P. *Telecult Power*. West Nyack, N.Y.: Parker Publishing, 1970.

Grillot De Givry, Emile. *The Illustrated Anthology of Sorcery Magic and Alchemy*. Translated by J. Courtenay Locke. New York: Causeway Books, 1973.

Manning, Al G. *The Miracle of Universal Psychic Power*. West Nyack, N.Y.: Parker Publishing, 1974.

MacIvor, Virginia and LaForest, Sandra. *Vibrations*. New York: Samuel Weiser, Inc., 1979.

Nichols, Beverly. *Powers That Be*. New York: Popular Library, 1966.

Nielsen, Greg and Polansky, Joseph. *Pendulum Power*. New York: Warner Books, 1977.

Ostrander, Sheila and Schroeder, Lynn. *Handbook of Psychic Discoveries*. New York: Berkley Publishing, 1974.

Russell, Edward W. *Report on Radionics*. Suffolk, U.K.: Neville Spearman, 1979.

Tansley, David V. *Dimensions in Radionics*. Devon, U.K.: Health Science Press, 1977.

Tansley, David V. *Radionics and the Subtle Anatomy of Man*. Whitstable, U.K.: Health Science Press, 1972.

White, John and Krippner, Stanley, ed. *Future Science*. New York: Doubleday, 1977.

EXTRA-TERRESTRIALS AMONG US
by George Andrews

According to a law already on the books, which may be activated whenever the government wishes to enforce it, anyone found guilty of E.T. contact is to be quarantined indefinitly under armed guard. Does that sound like the government doesn't take Extra-Terrestrials seriously? This book blows the lid off the government's cover-up about UFOs and their occupants, setting the stage for a "Cosmic Watergate."

Author George Andrews researched the evidence concerning extra-terrestrial intervention in human affairs for over a decade before presenting his startling conclusions.

You are given direct information as to *why* E.T.s are here, case history descriptions of their varying appearances, and what they are trying to accomplish. You will also learn how to determine whether an alien contact is beneficial or harmful. Human contacts are the vanguard of an experiment that will be expanded in our near future.

0-87542-010-9, 300 pgs. 5¼ x 8, photos, softcover $9.95

THE GOBLIN UNIVERSE
by Ted Holiday/Colin Wilson

Throughout history, we have been confronted with things that fail to fit squarely into our self-conceived reality. Many times we find them frightening. Even modern science is fearful and rejects those things for which it presently does not have any explanation—things like monsters, UFOs and the many things that go bump in the night.

It is the world of mind that is the Goblin Universe—goblin only because of our own limitations. And it is this greater universe that is the place of magick, of psychic phenomena, of ghosts and poltergeists, UFOs and the Men in Black, dragons and yetis and the Loch Ness Monster, of prophecy and retrogression and other mysteries.

Ted Holiday and Colin Wilson explore this amazing world with accounts of Ted Holiday's personal experiences and his search for a "unified theory" to open our perceptions to the universe. Wilson sees the problem in terms of the built-in nature of the human brain and our lack of training in its use.

0-87542-310-8, 288 pgs. 5¼ x 8, photos, softcover $9.95

LIFE FORCE
by Leo Ludzia

A secret, living energy—as ancient as the Pyramids, as modern as Star Wars. Since the beginning of time, certain people have known that there is this energy—a power that can be used by people for healing, magick, and spiritual development. It's been called many names: Huna, Orgone, Psionic, Prana, Kundalini, Odic force, Chi and others.

Leo Ludzia puts it all together in this amazing book *Life Force*. This is the first book which shows the histories and compares the theories and methods of *using* this marvelous energy. This force is available to us all, if only we know how to tap into it. Ludzia shows you how to make devices which will help you better use and generate this life force. This specialized information includes easy-to-follow directions on: how to build and use pyramids, orgone generators such as those used by Wilhelm Reich, and how to make and use the "Black Box" designed and used by the genious inventor T. G. Hieronymus.

0-87542-2437-6, 220 pgs., illus., mass market $3.95

CRYSTAL POWER
by Michael G. Smith

This is an amazing book, with complete instructions and diagrams so that *you* can make the master technology of ancient Atlantis: psionic (mind-controlled and life-energized machines) devices made from common quartz crystals!

You can easily construct an "Atlantean" Power Rod that can be used for healing or a weapon; or a Crystal Headband stimulating psychic powers; or a Time and Space Communications Generator; operated purely by your mind.

These crystal devices seem to work only with the disciplined mind power of a human operator, yet their very construction seems to start a process of growth and development, a new evolutionary step in the human psyche that bridges mind and matter.

0-87542-725-1, 288 pgs., illus., softcover $9.95

THE LLEWELLYN PRACTICAL GUIDE TO THE DEVELOPMENT OF PSYCHIC POWERS
by Denning and Phillips

You may not realize it, but . . . you already have the ability to use ESP, Astral Vision and Clairvoyance, Divination, Dowsing, Prophecy, Communications with Spirits, Mental Telepathy, etc. It's simply a matter of knowing what to do, and then to exercise (as with any talent) and develop them.

Written by two of the most knowledgeable experts in the world of Magic today, this book is a complete course—teaching you, step-by-step, how to develop these powers that actually have been yours since birth. Using the techniques they teach, you will soon be able to move objects at a distance, see into the future, know the thoughts and feelings of another person, find lost objects, locate water and even people using your own no-longer latent talents.

Psychic powers are as much a natural ability as any other talent. You'll learn to play with those new skills, work with groups of friends to accomplish things you never would have believed possible before reading this book.
0-87542-191-1, 256 pgs., 5¼ x 8, softcover $7.95

THE LLEWELLYN PRACTICAL GUIDE TO PSYCHIC SELF-DEFENSE AND WELL-BEING
by Denning and Phillips

Psychic Well-Being and Psychic Self-Defense are two sides of the same coin—just as physical health and resistance to disease are: each person (and every living thing) is surrounded by an electro-magnetic Force Field, or Aura, that can provide the means to Psychic Self-Defense and to dynamic Well-Being. This book explores the world of very real "psychic warfare" that we all are victims of.

This book shows the nature of genuine psychic attacks—ranging from actual acts of black magic to bitter jealousy and hate—and the reality of psychic stress. It shows how each person must develop his weakened aura into a powerful defense-shield—thereby gaining both physical protection and energetic well-being that can extend to protection from physical violence, accidents . . . even ill-health.
0-87542-190-3, 288 pgs., 5¼ x 8, softcover $7.95

THE LLEWELLYN PRACTICAL GUIDE
TO ASTRAL PROJECTION
by Denning and Phillips

Yes, your consciousness can be sent forth, out-of-the-body, with full awareness and return with full memory. You can travel through time and space, converse with non-physical entities, obtain knowledge by non-material means, and experience higher dimensions.

The reader is led through the essential stages for the inner growth and development that will culminate in fully conscious projection and return. Not only are the requisite practices set forth in step-by-step procedures, augmented with photographs and "puts-you-in-the-picture" visualization aids, but the vital reasons for undertaking them are clearly explained. Beyond this, the great benefits from the various practices themselves are demonstrated in renewed physical and emotional health, mental discipline, spiritual attainment, and the development of extra faculties.

0-87542-181-4, 239 pgs., 5¼ x 8, softcover $7.95

THE LLEWELLYN PRACTICAL GUIDE
TO CREATIVE VISUALIZATION
by Denning and Phillips

All things you will ever want must have their start in your mind. The average person uses very little of the full creative power that is potentially theirs.

Some people apply this innate power without actually knowing what they are doing, and achieve great success and happiness; most people, however, use this same power, again unknowingly, incorrectly, and experience bad luck, failure, or at best an unfulfilled life.

Through an easy series of step-by-step, progressive exercises, your mind is applied to bring desire into realization! Wealth, power, success, happiness . . . even psychic powers . . . all can be yours. You can easily develop this completely natural power, and correctly apply it, for your immediate and practical benefit.

0-87542-183-0, 255 pgs., 5¼ x 8, softcover.   **$7.95**

THE GODDESS BOOK OF DAYS
by Diane Stein

Diane Stein has created this wonderful guide to the Goddesses and festivals for every day of the year! This beautifully illustrated perpetual datebook will give you a listing for every day of the special Goddesses associated with that date along with plenty of room for writing in your appointments. It has over 100 illustrations of Goddesses from around the world.

0-87542-758-8, 300 pgs., hardbound, 5¼ x 8, illus. $12.95

THE LLEWELLYN ANNUALS

Llewellyn's MOON SIGN BOOK: approximately 400 pages of valuable information on gardening, fishing, weather, stock market forecasts, personal horoscopes, good planting dates, and general instructions for finding the best date to do just about anything! Articles by prominent forecasters and writers in the fields of gardening, astrology, politics, economics and cycles. This special almanac, different from any other, has been published annually since 1906.

State year $3.95

Llewellyn's SUN SIGN BOOK: Your personal horoscope for the entire year! All 12 signs are included in one handy book. Lucky dates are given for many activities for each sign. Monthly horoscopes by a prominent radio and TV astrologer for your personal Sun Sign. Articles on a variety of subjects written by well-known astrologers from around the country. Much more than just a horoscope guide! Entertaining and fun the year round.

State year $3.95

Llewellyn's DAILY PLANETARY GUIDE and Astrologer's Datebook: Includes all of the major daily aspects plus their exact times in Eastern and Pacific time zones, lunar phases, signs and voids plus their times, planetary motion, a monthly ephemeris, sunrise and sunset tables, special articles on the planets, signs, aspects, a business guide, planetary hours, rulerships, and much more. Large $5\frac{1}{4} \times 8$ format for more writing space, spiral bound to lay flat, address and phone listings, time zone conversion chart and blank horoscope chart.

State year $6.95

Llewellyn's ASTROLOGICAL CALENDAR: Large wall calendar of 52 pages. Beautiful full color cover and color inside. Includes special feature articles by famous astrologers, introductory information on astrology, Lunar Gardening Guide, celestial phenomena for the year, and monthly date pages which include aspects, lunar information, planetary motion, ephemeris, personal forecasts, lucky dates, planting and fishing dates, and more. 10 x 13 size. Set in Central time, with conversion table for other time zones worldwide.

State year $6.95